# The Architect's Portfolio

## planning, design, production

# Andreas Luescher

# The Architect's Portfolio

planning, design, production

Andreas Luescher

Routledge
Taylor & Francis Group

LONDON AND NEW YORK

First published 2010
by Routledge
2 Park Square, Milton Park, Abingdon, Oxon, OX14 4RN

Simultaneously published in the USA and Canada
by Routledge
711 Third Avenue, New York, Ny 10017

Routledge is an imprint of the Taylor & Francis Group, an
informa business

Typeset in Swiss 721 by Gavin Ambrose
Printed and bound in India by Replika Press Pvt. Ltd.

*British Library Cataloguing in Publication Data*
A catalogue record for this book is available from the
British Library

*Library of Congress Cataloging-in-Publication Data*
Luescher, Andreas.
The architect's portfolio : planning, design, production /
Andreas Luescher.
p. cm.
Includes bibliographical references and index.
1. Architecture portfolios—Design. I. Title.
NA1996.L84 2010
720.28—dc22
2009046080

ISBN13: 978-0-415-77901-2 (pbk)

# Contents

## Preface

The portfolio is a container used to ensure safe delivery of certain materials and ideas from one place to another, and from one time to another so we can communicate and share our best design work within the professional community of architects and prospective clients. While any portfolio, regardless of type or level of complexity, is a checkpoint in a dynamic process of development, the architect's portfolio is unique because it is – in all dimensions and concerns – architecture itself. It is structure and activity, in motion, and it is responsive to the effects of light. When considered this way a new range of expressive possibilities emerges. The goal of this book is to model theoretical and practical approaches to portfolio production which respond not only to specific application requirements but also to individual development and discovery. Some themes and concerns that run throughout this book are: portfolio as idea; designing for dialogue; framing narratives and deeper meaning; cultivation of image, beyond appearances; character, not style; reflective awareness, a different kind of self-portrait; designing for reception; and proportion (proportion is everything).

The analysis ranges from school application portfolio to job interview portfolio, bearing in mind that in each case one must make unique choices about self-presentation, which lead to potentially different manifestations of a single body of work. After a brief look at the background of portfolio development, the book examines the steps in the planning, design, production, and presentation of architecture portfolios.

## Contextualize It

Chapter 1 offers a brief, highly subjective timeline of architectural portfolios starting with the 1507 *portmanteau*, continuing with the first self-described 'Porto Folio' in 1722 by J. Richardson, Marcel Duchamp's Box in a Valise, and the eccentric portfolios of Albert Kner and Charles Eames. The aim here is to diffuse the notion of 'originality' and place it in a continuum of development over centuries. By doing so, readers can find unlimited sources of inspiration, models, and bridges to alternative ways of thinking about portfolio-making. It is hoped this will help them to negotiate through derivatives to original sources and then to create more confident design solutions of their own. Also stressed is the importance and value of acknowledging sources.

## Plan It, Select It

Chapter 2 describes planning in terms of routines of thinking: reasoning, capturing essences, perceiving, knowing, and caring. It lays out a series of rules and guidelines, while making it clear that these are a starting point, a foundation, not a set of limitations.

## Design It, Produce It

Chapter 3 addresses ideas and techniques that go into portfolio-making. Parts make up a cohesive whole, big issues are solved first, subtleties come later. Attention is paid to the multi-sensory qualities of architecture that can be transcribed to the portfolio medium, including the language of materials, physicality, and impressions beyond specific information.

## Send It, Present It, Market It

Chapter 4 approaches presentation as a relationship between internal and external structure. Practical strategies for maximizing exposure to a specific and/or general audience are discussed in terms of long- and short-range goals. Criteria for self-assessment  focus on learning and discovering that where one portfolio ends the next begins.

## Case Studies

I invited firms and individuals to describe in pictures and words their own portfolio-making process. The self-reflective nature of this task produced a wealth of practical templates, theoretical preferences, and highly personal insights. The retrospective summaries in the case studies allow us the opportunity to see individuals organize, direct, and reflect on their strategies for their portfolios, including idea-generation techniques, creative direction issues, and the evaluation of media components. Readers will find a wide range of invention, philosophy, formality, media, and intentions formulated by the contributors. The candour and generosity of the contributors are unmistakable.

# 1
# Contextualize It

## Contextualize It

The portfolio is a container and a vehicle, the specific contents of which change to reflect the momentary intention of the presenter based on the perceived needs of the receiver. All portfolios – across diverse cultural settings, populations, and other contexts – are attempts to convey the essence of a person's character and work rather than just the facts of his/her life. In its application of the ethic of selectivity to raw accumulation, the portfolio shares a venerable tradition of self-interpretation and self-presentation with the autobiography, a distinct literary genre that arose in the 17th century in a world being transformed by urbanization, mobility, literacy, communications, and Renaissance notions of individuality.

Set within a broad historical context it becomes immediately clear that self-presentation and marketing have been dual motives for architects to make portfolios since the 18th century. Knowing something of the history of portfolio making – which is very rich and represents a very cultivated world – helps architecture students and emerging professionals discover notions of originality and find unlimited sources of fascination, information, models, and bridges to historical ideas within and outside the discipline of architecture. Those findings help the portfolio maker adapt to diverse forms and a variety of contexts. The outcome results in a richer portfolio which will demonstrate his/her own creative originality, and impress potential employers and clients. Even more importantly, the knowledge gained will support the creator to find his/her way through derivatives to original sources and then to more confident design solutions. As a collection of visual information the portfolio is a presentation format perfectly matched to a global culture increasingly measured out in images. It is a locus for the transmission of ideals, values, and, if nothing else, norms. It is also a methodology of self-discovery using intellectual and imaginative development in the context of the designer's work. The portfolio is the (potential) locus of critical description/representation.

To approach an understanding of current portfolio planning, design and production, we can look at notable examples of the past and consider the factors that were influential in their development. By examining landmarks in the evolving nature and use of the portfolio we see connections to many other fields – including package design, exhibition design, advertising, product development – and the important relationship between content and container. What follows is a selective list illustrating the evolution of the portfolio emphasizing its existence as a (portable) structure around which activity is organized.

## 1.1 Portfolio as Autobiography

Autobiography is the induction of the viewer into the writer's world. As a cultivator of self-consciousness and self-representation the portfolio can be compared to the autobiography which emerged as a distinct literary form during the 17th century along with empirical science and inductive method. An ideology of self-examination, which departed radically from the view of lives in archetypal terms, as in St Augustine's *City of God* (completed AD 426), was transmitted by this new form of representation. Like the autobiography, the portfolio operates as a matrix for intellectual exploration and self-assessment, placing the value of an individual's incremental output within the greater context of learning to think.

The *portmanteau* preceded the first self-described portfolio by 200 years. The first noted reference was made in 1507 to a ranking French officer who 'carries a mantle of a person in high position'. Did 'mantle' describe a cloak or deportment – the way one carries oneself, presents oneself? In France during the 16th century, the portmanteau was a person – an officer in the king's service who carried (Fr. *porter*, carry, transmit, transfer something) the royal mantle (*manteau*) of the king when travelling. The mantle was of great value and was accordingly carried in a case of soft leather. Eventually, in England, the case itself became the portmanteau and was used as a travelling bag for carrying various articles.

The cultural significance of the portfolio coincided with transformations in social organization brought about by urbanization, easier travel, and faster communications. As a collection of visual information the portfolio was a presentation format perfectly matched to an early modern world increasingly mediated by images. The first self-described portfolio was Jonathan Richardson's *An Account of Some of the Statues, Bas-reliefs, Drawings, and Pictures in Italy* (1722) – a collection of *veduta* ('souvenir views') intended to give a sense of access to a new and expanding world. It functioned like a portfolio but was used as a guidebook by young Englishmen making the Grand Tour.

Palladio's 1570 *Quattro Libri dell' Architettura* (Four Books of Architecture) – as much catalogue as scholarly disquisition – was arguably the first architectural pattern book, a genre which was widespread in Europe from the 16th century and in Europe and America from the 17th to 19th centuries. *Quattro Libri dell' Architettura* can be placed under two broad categories: the monograph, showcasing designs of a particular architect, and the manual of ideal designs and details intended for builders and craftworkers who wanted to be kept up-to-date.

The Red Books of English author and landscape designer Humphry Repton (1752–1818) are another good example of the crossover between a monograph and a manual. Repton's recommendations to clients on the improvement of their estates were elegantly bound in red morocco leather, hence the term 'Red Books'. Repton coined the term 'slide' to denote an illustration technique used to great effect in the Red Books. Slides made ingenious use of overlays or paper flaps to enchantingly transform a 'before' setting into an 'after' or improved view.

Architectural pattern books, like the portfolio, had a utility which transcended disciplinary boundaries and developmental hierarchies. Their dual existence as autobiography and marketing tool can be mapped and found in many different forms of literature.

## 1.2 Portfolio as Portable Museum

Part documentary and part interview the portfolio is like a dimension offering opportunities for assessment of one's work in a context of professional and intellectual growth. The genesis of the portfolio and its diversification (as noun and verb) are examined (briefly) for what can be revealed about the intentions and effects of self-expression/ self-promotion in our current commercial culture. The portfolio as a thing coincides with the modern cultural response to a world being drastically altered by shifts in population, and advances in transportation and communications.

The portfolio of today is a showcase for highly individual designers and architects. In this context it is worth mentioning the portfolio approach of Marcel Duchamp (1887–1968) which preserved his legacy as one of the most influential artists of the modern era. Duchamp's 'portable museum', his Box in a Valise (1942–54), was a sophisticated portfolio that was a resumé of Duchamp's life in art, created with painstaking care in the face of a vanishing material legacy. In his Box he constructed a system of horizontal and vertical lines simulating a perfectly scaled room instead of presenting its contents in the linear sequence of a book. Marcel Duchamp's portfolio is more about performance than arrangement of the reproductions or the mere collection of information as a cosmetic arrangement of loose pieces of work in a folder. The Box, like the autobiography, validates the idea that data and details must be gathered before general conclusions can be drawn or any overarching pattern 'seen' (see Figure 1). It is also the synthesis of Duchamp's paradoxical principles of cross-references through assembling photographs, supervising colour reproduction and manifold overlaps of his works. These apparently contradictory rationales are reflected in the quality of the craftsmanship used to make his miniaturized objects which acted as a catalyst for the public

**Figure 1**
Marcel Duchamp (French, 1887–1968),
*Boîte-en-valise [The box in a valise]* 1942-54
cardboard and wooden box containing
replicas and reproductions of works by Duchamp
closed 7.9 h x 35.5 w x 39.5 d cm
approx. size open 35.5 h x 140.0 w x 7.9 d cm
National Gallery of Australia, Canberra
Purchased 1979

Digital image © Marcel Duchamp. Licensed by ADAGP,
France & ARS, New York

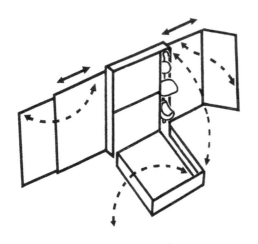

**Figure 2**
Opening mechanism and moving parts of the box

**Figure 3**
Front of the briefcase
**Figure 4**
Inside the briefcase

Jean Tinguely (Swiss, 1925–91), *Méta* (1973), text
by K. G. Pontus Hultén, published by Pierre Horay
Editeur, Paris. Briefcase with lock closure and
handle containing photolithographs of drawings,
diagrams, photographs, and newspaper clippings,
transparent vellums, and an original painting
executed by Tinguely's machine, 'Meta-matic no.
6'.

Digital Image © Toledo Art Museum/Licensed by Artists Rights Society
(ARS), New York.

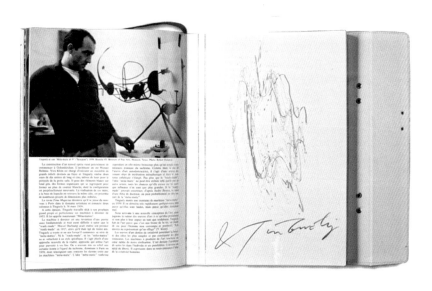

response almost like the open and shut positions of a medieval triptych.

Essentially, the portfolio model is a testament to the value of repetition. For example, the Swiss kinetic artist Jean Tinguely (1925–91) made his first portfolio to simulate a briefcase with lock and carrying handle, and containing an original 'Meta-matic' drawing (see Figures 2, 3, and 4). In this portfolio he used overlays and fold-outs to illustrate his exhaustive research for the historic 'Machine' exhibition at the Museum of Modern Art (1960). The portfolio resembles Tinguely's 'meta-mechanical' devices, which draw, move, play, fight, explode, and/or erupt. It is characterized by a patterned recurrence of elements or motifs at regular or irregular intervals based on his abstract spatial constructions.

In the end Tinguely's portfolio is more than about looking good: it provides a record – both mechanical and imaginative – and, more importantly, it provides a manifesto that reflects the value of Tinguely's artistic endeavour.

## 1.3 Portfolio of Games

The portfolio is characterized by or productive of new things or new ideas: it is creative, innovative, innovatory, inventive, and original. Examples of eccentric portfolios are Albert Kner's 'Portfolio of Games' and Charles Eames's 'House of Cards' which contain unusual elements that both distinguish the format and serve as part of the message and are creative, informative, surprising, and original artistic endeavours.

Hungarian designer Albert Kner (1899–1976) created portfolios which were highly flexible instruments of entertainment and adaptable to diverse use. In all, he crafted 15 dazzling individual booklets and a slipcase that made up his 'Portfolio of Games'. Kner's work showed in great detail the processes and strategies involved in writing, solving a problem, researching a topic, analysing information, and describing his own observations in the construction of a portfolio.

Kner's complex constructions were made of wood, paper, and metal. He illustrated and painted intricate and imaginative detail on the board games. He and his family migrated to Chicago and, at his second interview with Walter Paepack of Container Corporation of America (CCA), he was hired on the spot as CCA's first package designer, showing the benefits of his unusual approach to the portfolio.

In his 'House of Cards' (1952) – made up of two decks of fifty-four playing-card size cards – Charles Eames created three-dimensional structures and promoted the idea that a portfolio can act as a game too. Eames demonstrated how the design and presentation of information, with an emphasis on 3D form, need not diminish the role of substance, skill, emotional content, worldview, or appropriateness.

The cards are very appealing not only on a purely sensory level – at a closer look they reveal messages about the everyday objects we take for granted but no longer see as useful and beautiful. In its truest form the interplay with the cards is like the process of developing a portfolio: it is essential to ensure the continued life of the portfolio by adding to and refining its contents.

## 1.4 Case Studies

The 21st century is witnessing the shift from print technology to digital reproduction. The case studies in this chapter illustrate portfolio compositions that reflect innovations of mobility, transferability, and hybrid methods – the effects of broader processes of globalized production and communication rather than outcomes of disciplinary change. They are Kevin Le's visionary 3D portfolio, Filippo Lodi's 4D compositional portfolio, Che-Wei Wang's interactive web portfolio, Ceri Williams's performance-oriented portfolio, and Richard M. Wright's portfolio collaboration between teacher and student.

**Kevin Le** stresses productive and engaging dialogue as the mission of the portfolio. His method is designed to engender open-ended relationships between presenter and audience. Clients can be strongly involved by making decisions that must be considered, delineated, and adjusted. He pays attention to the balance of the reception side of the equation with the presentation side. He encourages the involvement of clients in the decision-making process by formatting for minimal bias, openness to discussion, and invention.

**Filippo Lodi**'s portfolio programme is laid out as a scientific diagram of neurotransmitters and catalysts. These so-called reactions offer options for both linear and non-linear navigation through the portfolio composition. His ability to organize the flow of information according to hierarchies, matrices, series, overlays, spatial issues, and parallel texts makes his portfolio unique.

**Che-Wei Wang**'s notion of inter-temporality – the relationship between past, present, and future events or conditions – can be seen in his close, precise, almost romantic examination of time-keeping devices. The discrete elements of his portfolio process are documented with precise stillness like the momentary suspension of the second hand of a clock.

**Ceri Williams**'s refreshing informality and easy confidence are readable at a glance. He works purposely against a field of standardized, impersonal, manufactured portfolios (as containers) to create intentionally self-descriptive portfolios. His working method and its results are at the same time unpretentious, low key, and explicitly friendly and outgoing.

**Richard M. Wright** conceptualizes the hybrid portfolio as an experiential field in which trajectories are devised to make projects with no physical or graphical sense of connection. This is accomplished not only through different techniques of environmental representation but also through a common investment in immersion, mobility, and experiential novelty.

# Kevin Le

## Strategy

The aim of this portfolio approach is to allow the author to learn, and grow from his/her work; to recognize common threads and ideas, to make distinctions about them, and to understand their importance; and to better understand oneself as a designer, while at the same time providing a method in explaining our work in a succinct manner to others. I believe this method is advantageous for intuitive designers who make design decisions based more on feel than reason. It allows this internal 'feeling' to be externalized and move from emotion to logic. I would add that this approach would be more suited in situations where the portfolio is shown with the author present allowing for an interactive dialogue. It also allows for projects of different categories to be compared and dissected, like paintings and buildings or sculptures. The portfolio consists of multiple individual panels that allow for projects to be grouped in various sequences and allow for an individual panel to be studied next to another panel or in isolation.

Deciding on a size panel has many factors associated with it. I personally find that a square format is appropriate for this type of portfolio. Square panels have some drawbacks to them, but the benefits outweigh their shortcomings. Their equal sides provide a non bias on gravity, that is to say, the square nature allows the author to look at his/her work upside down, turned 90° clockwise or counter-clockwise, and still be weighted equally. Looking at your work from a different vantage point can potentially allow for new readings or observations about the project. Its non-directionality allows the inherent forces to become more apparent.

## Production

Materiality is an important factor for the portfolio. This component is a more dynamic one that allows for the same freedom of exploration usually found at the beginning of projects, but now applied at the 'conclusion'. This is the notion of having the liberty to make marks over your finished work to better understand, to explore another idea, to develop ideas and to explain ideas without the fear of ruining your finished product. It is the same concept as tracing paper or layering in Photoshop. It is the dry erase marker applied to clear plexiglas.

Some practical issues arise that are intrinsic to this approach: ease of transporting many components; protection of the plexiglas from scratching; need for an orderly and well thought-out arrangement. A container is one solution to this problem. Many material choices are available for this task. I feel that wood is the most appropriate due to its malleable and rich nature. I prefer the feel and smell of unfinished wood. A box is built with the same character as the panels, and stainless steel hinges provide the opening for this container. Individual slats of wood provide slots for the panels and give them separation from the hardware on the panels. A trough is carved around the container to provide a groove for a thick rubber band that secures the lid. Additional ruts are carved out for storing the dry erase markers. The container is personalized with a seal, emblem, or fingerprint.

**Advice**
- Make sure the portfolio type matches its intended use. Whether it is for a face-to-face interview or for an anonymous viewing the portfolio should enable the author to take full advantage of the circumstances.
- Technology is changing rapidly, staying current will create new opportunities. Be careful not to substitute IT for the skills and lessons you developed in your art class.
- Do not be afraid to experiment; good things will come out of play.
- Every problem or issue that arises is an opportunity for a creative and appropriate solution.
- Have fun.

**case study**

hardware

what m
I thi

Concept diagrams

an e

Project sentence press on left

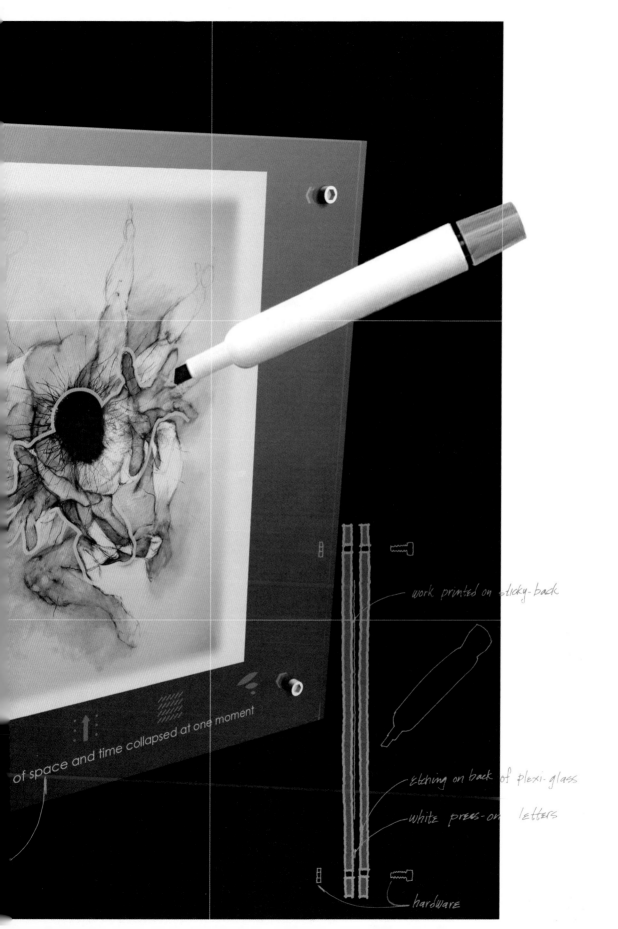

of space and time collapsed at one moment

work printed on sticky-back

etching on back of plexi-glass

white press-on letters

hardware

slots for dry erase markers

rubber band

## Filippo Lodi

**1.**
**What are the nuts and bolts of your portfolio-production?**
I think of my portfolio as a device that frames the time and the space of my work, the space of production. I therefore try to transform it into an intelligent system that aims at sectioning and measuring a variable extract of myself. As today's pervasive data-streaming reality trains us to filter information, the portfolio as a frame of my own data flow must highlight different aspects and target the strongest points of each project. My portfolio adapts the contents of each project to an overall framed content that inscribes the space of production.

**2.**
**Is your portfolio designed as a summation of your current preoccupations or is it designed as a continuum of your work as a whole?**
I must be constantly reshaping and restructuring patterns of my portfolio as an interactive device, as an object that subverts the fast-food-like methods of communication that dominate and condition our way of reading things, forcing a ubiquitous simplicity as if we could not read more than a 'twitter' message. It is a fuzzy object.

**3.**
**Do you keep many portfolios? What distinguishes one from another?**
My portfolio is a system that adapts to who will read it. It can be transformed in format, size and medium – it can be digital, a website, or simply remain usable in a short version.

**4.**

**Does the physical environment of the portfolio agree with its contents or does it provide meaningful opposition?**

The printed version creates a set of design issues that refer to the senses. The type and size of paper, type of printer, how the paper is bonded together – just like a structural element, it has to be designed. The ability to reproduce the same images in a portfolio allows for a great capacity of production and the possibility to produce constantly differing objects that belong to the same family.

**5.**

**Do you use materials of which your designs are made?**

The outside skin of the object portfolio is the container of the content portfolio. It does not illustrate any content but rather it highlights the value of what is contained within it – it is designed.

**6.**

**Do you have any advice about your portfolio-making process?**

Read:

http://en.wikipedia.org/wiki/Empire_(book).

**case study**

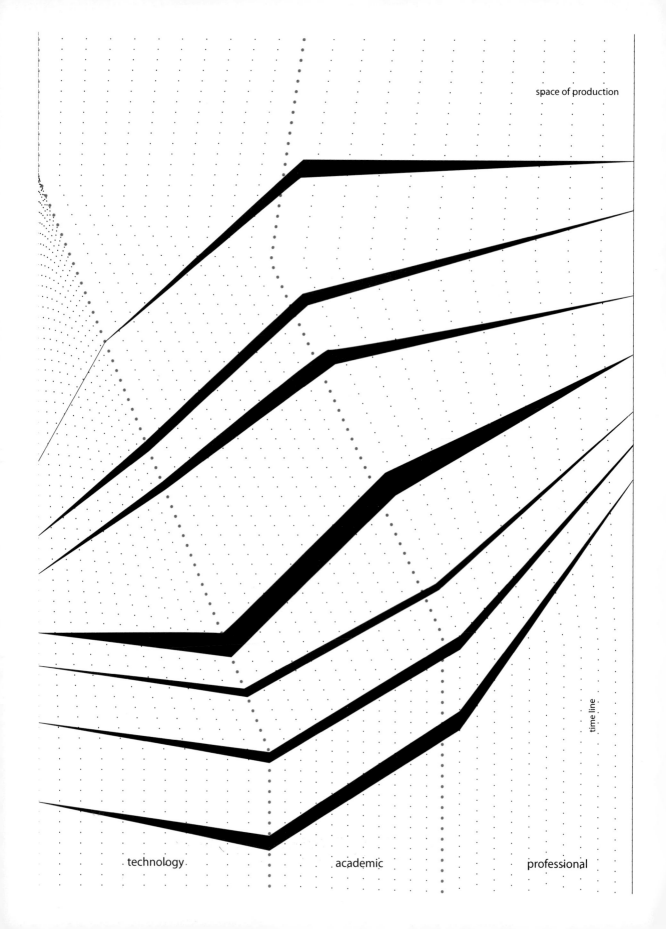

space of production

time line

technology     academic     professional

**filippo lodi**
portfolio

project 01

project 02

project 03

project 04

project 05

project 06

project 07

portfolio network

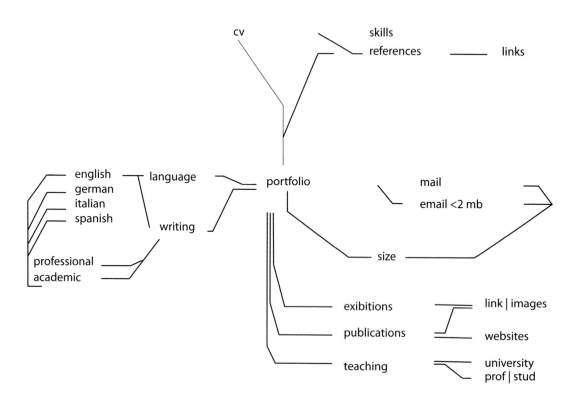

cv

skills
references ——— links

english —— language —— portfolio
german                          mail
italian                         email <2 mb
spanish
            writing
professional
academic                        size

                                exibitions        link | images
                                publications      websites
                                teaching          university
                                                  prof | stud

portfolio content, layout, cover

main page|layout

header

image

text | diagram

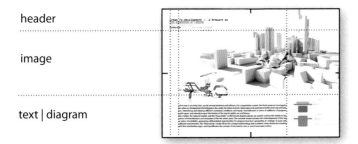

content pages

rendering
plans
urban plan
maquette

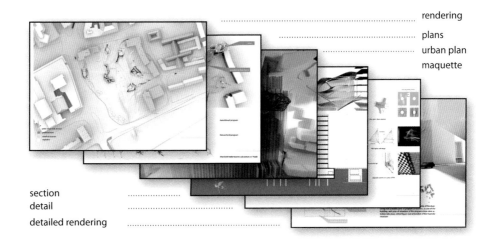

section
detail
detailed rendering

cover

# Che-Wei Wang

**1.**
**What are the nuts and bolts of your portfolio-production?**
The portfolio for me is a document that evolves along with each project. It is a small booklet that acts as a companion to each project containing sketches, diagrams, and text all meant for internal use. Just as the project goes through many iterations, so does the booklet. By the completion of each project, the document naturally gets refined to reflect and represent the work as a portfolio.

**2.**
**What are your inspirations and influences?**
My work and the representation of the work are strongly influenced by the possibilities that technology offers. New ways to print, publish, and interact with media excite me.

**3.**
**How would you describe your portfolio-making process?**
I like to think that I can freely explore, discover, and create like an artist through hundreds of iterations as a project evolves and find the right moment to discipline the work through the eyes of an architect. The portfolio is the platform on which one can freely wander and momentarily step back to evaluate, select, qualify, and nurture work into the next round of explorations.

**4.**
**Do you keep many portfolios? What distinguishes one from another?**
I keep a lot of portfolios in various shapes, sizes, and media. More recent portfolios are booklets of individual projects. But even those are not uniform. Each opportunity to create a portfolio comes along with a new set of ideas. Maybe, one day, the format will be perfected and all project booklets will follow the same format and design, but so far it's been a learning process.

**5.**
**Is your portfolio designed as a summation of your current preoccupations or is it designed as a continuum of your work as a whole?**
The portfolio is more focused on my current preoccupations. There is always something new and exciting to work on right around the corner, so I spend most of my time thinking about what's next rather than what I've done and how it might relate to what's next.

**6.**

**Is your portfolio a stream-of-consciousness, incorporating whatever contributes to your feelings without necessarily having any particular literal meaning in relation to the material?**

My portfolio often acts like a sketchbook for a stream of ideas and concerns. I literally use the draft prints of the booklet as a place to sketch.

**7.**

**Is your portfolio designed for flexibility?**

The online portfolio is extremely flexible. Projects are added and edited continuously. I try to use print as flexibly as I can, but each portfolio reaches a moment when it is complete as an archive for a project or set of projects.

**8.**

**Is your portfolio primarily image-based or is it primarily text-based?**

It's primarily image-based. Text is there as support material. There are some instances where the text is crucial to understanding the context or history of the project but, in most cases, the images take the lead.

**9.**

**Is your portfolio primarily design-driven or is it primarily project-driven?**

It is primarily project driven. Projects of different scales and circumstances require different approaches, so I have only a very loose overarching philosophy that guides all the design choices. Each project demands a portfolio for itself.

case study

Each project is accompanied by a booklet that evolves throughout the design process. Early draft booklets provide a sketch platform that functions as a design tool that transitions into the final presentation.

Over the course of 4 months, six experimental time keeping devices were built. The booklet titled *Time in Six Parts* reveals the conceptual framework for each piece and provides documentation through text and images.

Beginning with the earliest version, 5.5" x 8.5" draft booklets are mocked up from cover to cover. They provide printed proofs to be red-lined and blank pages to be filled with sketch layout. Quick mock ups take the book out of the computer so that it can be continuously evaluated as a tangible object.

 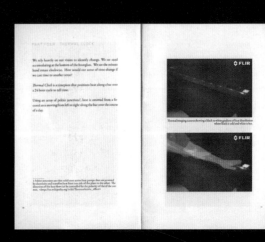

draft layout                                                                                                    nearing final

How accurate does a clock need to be?  Most household clocks display time with 3 mechanical movements; the hour, on a 12 hour cycle; minutes past the hour; and seconds past the minute. How crucial is it for us to know how many seconds are past the minute?  Do we need to know the exact number of minutes past the hour?

*One Hour Sprocket* is a wall-mounted 12 hour clock with a 60 tooth sprocket attached to a motor, completing one revolution every hour.  From the sprocket hangs a chain that consists of 720 links.  Each link accounts for every minute of a 12 hour cycle. Among the black chain links is one polished stainless steel link to identify the position of the hour past 12 o'clock.  To tell time one can estimate the position of the "hour hand" or count the number of links from the polished link to the top of the clock for a more accurate reading.

Between two 1/4" steel plates, sits a stepper motor, which ticks every 18 seconds.  The hanging chain jiggles with each tick reassuring the clock's functionality.

Image and text adjustments take place in printed book form so the gutter can be taken into consideration.  Each timepiece is laid out over two spreads.  The second spread contains more supporting images.

final booklet

**cwwang.com** runs on Wordpress. The open source software (written in PHP and CSS) provides an intuitive back-end allowing projects and related posts to be easily added, keeping the site current. The frontend is controlled by a custom theme titled Hemingwei (a modified version of Hemingway by Kyle Neath). All the visual elements on the frontend are easily adjusted through edits in PHP and CSS on a continuous basis as small design changes are made rather than a complete design overhaul every few months.

cwwang.com | Che-Wei Wang

### 3.16 Billion Cycles

Can we watch decay? Can we see glass as a fluid slowly slumping and deforming over time? Everything is in constant flux, yet we consider many things around us static and fixed. 3.16 Billion Cycles is an attempt to unravel a seemingly unchanging 100 years into a set of relationships in digestible increments.

(more...)

full post>>

Posted at 4pm on 05/05/09 | 8 comments
Filed Under: Featured, Mechanisms, Physical Computing, Products, Projects, Sculpture, Time

**links on del.icio.us**

Download Create Booklet PDF Service for Mac - Export documents as a PDF booklet. MacUpdate Mac Author Tools Software Downloads
THE CLASS « Bamboo Bike Studio
KINETICA MUSEUM OF KINETIC ART : Spitalfields London
Sliding House, By DRMM | Video | Wallpaper* Magazine
Gizmodo – Jaquet Droz Time-Writing Machine: Elegant in Still Life, Clumsy on Video – jaquet droz
TOKYO FIBER '09 SENSEWARE

**Other Work**

core.form-ula
Future Feeder
Journal of Architecture and Computation Culture
momobots
on Flickr
on Vimeo
Prefab China

**About**

cwwang.com is where you will find Che-Wei Wang's latest projects, blog posts, and other things. If you have my business card, fold it into a paper airplane.

[twitter.com/sayway]

my location last updated 05.08.09 12:58 am.
[bigger map]
cell tracking by InstaMapper

**Recent Posts**

05.06 — Thermal Clock
05.05 — Cinematic Timepiece
05.03 — Time in Six Parts
05.03 — Counting to a Billion
05.01 — 3.16 Billion Cycles
04.01 — Sprocket Rhinoscript
03.21 — 1 Hour Sprocket Clock
03.26 — Sun Angle Script
02.14 — In a Lifetime
01.07 — momo <3 sparkfun
12.23 — Thermochromic Slow Resolution Display
12.11 — 21st Century Confession Booth
12.07 — I can't stop thinking of you (too)
11.26 — P.Life V2
11.20 — Elevator P
11.07 — Turf Bombing
10.23 — The New Vote

**Categories**

All Posts
Projects
2D Graphics (12)
Architecture (17)
Arduino (13)
Big Screens (2)
C (14)
Comp Form (16)
Featured (9)
Furniture (9)
GUI AJAX (1)
ITP (75)
Live Web (6)
Mechanisms (2)
Media Change (3)
moMo (15)
Oblik (8)
openFrameworks (5)
Ornos (4)
Parametric Modeling (6)
Physical Computing (41)
Press (6)
Processing (12)
Products (19)
Rhinoscript (10)
Sculpture (7)
Soft Pneumatic Exoskeleton (8)
Software (22)
Teaching (9)
Telepresence (9)
Tetherlight (3)
Time (8)
Uncategorized (1)
Urban Computing (7)
Video (4)
Wearables (12)
Web (8)
Work in Progress (87)

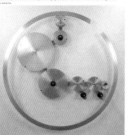

Each project expands into its own page revealing more details. Below each project, visitors can provide feedback and post questions. Other websites that link to the page are automatically added as comments, providing visitors with relevant links.

The projects page is one long scrollable, chronological list of projects.

# Ceri Williams

## Strategy

I approached the tasks of compiling and presenting my portfolio as an opportunity to make a personal record of my work. This allowed me to concentrate on archiving the material in a way that best reflects the characters of my designs. I avoided tailoring the portfolio for a single specific purpose.

I chose the European A3 format (420mm wide x 297mm high; a manageable size to carry), allowing inexpensive and accessible printing, and quick re-arrangement when necessary. Designing the carry-case, layout, and labelling gave me an opportunity to be the maker and to steer clear of the typical hard-edged black folder with laminated pages.

The pages are kept loose so that sheets can be replaced, augmented, or removed as necessary. The loose leaves allow the pages to be viewed side by side. A wide range of architectural work is included. The relationship of some of the projects to architecture may not always be immediately obvious.

A simple layout – usually just one image per A3 page, with generous borders and simple labelling – is applied throughout the portfolio, although this styling is, on occasions, modified. Specific weights and colours of paper are chosen to best suit the character of each project.

Labelling of images is done using stamped and handwritten stickers. I chose a simple motif for each project and handmade a rubber stamp to print each label. As well as providing information, the labels make the component sheets for each project recognizable, and they help to impose the uncomplicated organization I intended.

The final part of my portfolio has individual photographs attached to the back of each sheet. A desire to help the viewer gain an insight into the contextual inspiration behind a particular drawing led me to take a series of photographs that depict existing sites. Buildings, objects, materials, and transitions between these elements have been photographed.

## Production

I constructed a simple, wooden, hinged box in which to store the sheets. The box is robust and can easily be carried to interviews. An interest in screenprinting and textiles led me to cover the case in fabric printed with one of my designs. (The fabric lies over padding.) The size and tactile nature of the case is intriguing and encourages people to open it, and then examine its contents with care.

My intention, during all the stages of the portfolio's making, was to derive enjoyment from the process and minimize the need for any specialist or costly production techniques. While being careful not to detract from the portfolio being perceived as a single and thorough body of work, I favour the minor inconsistencies that result from these handmade methods.

## Advice

In compiling my portfolio I considered it important to reflect the character not only of my work, but also of myself as an individual designer. Just as a minimalist drawing would look out of place if presented in an ornate gilt frame, staying faithful to a particular stylistic approach becomes highly significant when compiling a portfolio.

In the presentation of a full body of work, care should be taken to avoid conflicting and confusing methods of presentation. In this way, the common themes and elements of design – that may not otherwise be immediately perceived – are made evident.

**case study**

I APPROACHED THE TASKS OF COMPILING AND PRESENTING MY PORTFOLIO AS AN OPPORTUNITY TO MAKE A PERSONAL RECORD OF MY WORK. THIS ALLOWED ME TO CONCENTRATE ON ARCHIVING THE MATERIAL IN A WAY THAT BEST REFLECTS THE CHARACTERS OF MY DESIGNS. I AVOIDED TAILOR-ING THE PORTFOLIO FOR A SINGLE SPECIFIC PURPOSE.

I CHOSE THE EUROPEAN A3 FORMAT (420mm WIDE BY 297mm HIGH; A MANAGEABLE SIZE TO CARRY), ALLOWING INEXPENSIVE AND ACCESSIBLE PRINTING, AND QUICK RE-ARRANGEMENT WHEN NECESSARY. DESIGNING THE CARRY-CASE, LAYOUT AND LABELLING GAVE ME THE CHANCE TO BE THE MAKER AND TO STEER CLEAR OF THE TYPICAL HARD-EDGED BLACK FOLDER.

THE PAGES ARE KEPT LOOSE SO THAT SHEETS CAN BE REPLACED, AUGMENTED, OR REMOVED AS NECESSARY. THE LOOSE LEAVES ALLOW THE PAGES TO BE VIEWED SIDE BY SIDE. A WIDE RANGE OF PROJECTS WERE INCLUDED.

1.

A SIMPLE LAYOUT — USUALLY JUST ONE IMAGE PER A3 PAGE, WITH GENEROUS BORDERS AND SIMPLE LABELLING — IS APPLIED THROUGHOUT THE PORTFOLIO, ALTHOUGH THIS STYLING IS, ON OCCASIONS, MODIFIED. SPECIFIC WEIGHTS AND COLOURS OF PAPER ARE CHOSEN TO BEST SUIT THE CHARACTER OF EACH PROJECT.

PRINTED IMAGE

LABEL

LABELLING OF IMAGES IS DONE USING STAMPED AND HANDWRITTEN STICKERS. I CHOSE A SIMPLE MOTIF FOR EACH PROJECT AND HAND-MADE A RUBBER STAMP TO PRINT EACH LABEL. AS WELL AS PROVIDING INFORMATION, THE LABELS MAKE THE COMPONENT SHEETS FOR EACH PROJECT RECOGNISABLE, AND THEY HELP TO IMPOSE THE UNCOMPLICATED ORGANISATION.

2.

LONG SECTION CUT THROUGH ACCESS WALKWAYS IN 'TRENCH'

PEN & INK WASH WITH PHOTOSHOP

ORIGINAL: 2000 x 700mm

Ceri Williams statemodern@hotmail.com

FASHION SCHOOL WOVEN INTO DIVERSE AND PREVIOUSLY UNDESIRABLE CONTEXT OF ROAD, WALKWAY, UNDERPASS AND BRIDGE NETWORK.

PEN & INK WASH

ORIGINAL: 800 x 500 mm

Ceri Williams statemodern@hotmail.com

3.

THE FINAL PART OF MY PORTFOLIO HAS INDIVIDUAL PHOTOGRAPHS ATTACHED TO THE BACK OF EACH SHEET. A DESIRE TO RE-CONTEXTUALISE THE INSPIRATION BEHIND PARTICULAR DRAWINGS LED ME TO TAKE A SERIES OF PHOTOGRAPHS THAT DEPICT EXISTING SITES. BUILDINGS, OBJECTS, MATERIALS AND TRANSITIONS BETWEEN THESE ELEMENTS HAVE BEEN PHOTOGRAPHED.

4.

I CONSTRUCTED A SIMPLE, WOODEN, HINGED BOX IN WHICH TO STORE THE SHEETS. THE BOX IS ROBUST AND CAN EASILY BE CARRIED TO INTERVIEWS. AN INTEREST IN SCREEN-PRINTING AND TEXTILES LED ME TO COVER THE CASE IN FABRIC PRINTED WITH ONE OF MY DESIGNS. (THE FABRIC LIES OVER A SOFT PADDING). THE SIZE AND TACTILE NATURE OF THE CASE IS INTRIGUING AND ENCOURAGES PEOPLE TO OPEN IT, AND THEN EXAMINE ITS CONTENTS WITH CARE

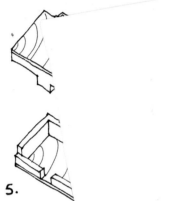

5.

MY INTENTION DURING ALL THE STAGES OF THE PORTFOLIO'S MAKING, WAS TO DERIVE ENJOYMENT FROM THE PROCESS AND MINIMISE THE NEED FOR ANY SPECIALIST OR COSTLY PRODUCTION TECHNIQUES. WHILE BEING CAREFULL NOT TO DETRACT FROM THE PORTFOLIO BEING PERCEIVED AS A SINGLE AND THOROUGH BODY OF WORK, I FAVOUR THE MINOR INCONSISTENCIES THAT RESULTS FROM THESE HANDMADE METHODS.

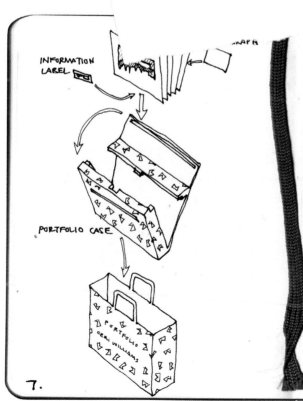

INFORMATION LABEL

PORTFOLIO CASE

7.

IN COMPILING MY PORTFOLIO I CONSIDERED IT IMPORTANT TO REFLECT THE CHARACTER NOT ONLY OF MY WORK BUT ALSO OF MYSELF AS AN INDIVIDUAL DESIGNER. JUST AS A MINIMILIST DRAWING WOULD LOOK OUT OF PLACE IF PRESENTED IN AN ORNATE GILT FRAME, STAYING FAITHFUL TO A PARTICULAR STYLISTIC APPROACH BECOMES HIGHLY STYLISTIC APPROACH BECOMES HIGHLY SIGNIFICANT WHEN COMPILING A PORTFOLIO.

IN THE PRESENTATION OF A FULL BODY OF WORK, CARE SHOULD BE TAKEN TO AVOID CONFLICTING AND CONFUSING METHODS OF PRESENTATION. IN THIS WAY, THE COMMON THEMES AND ELEMENTS OF DESIGN – THAT MAY NOT OTHERWISE BE IMMEDIATELY PERCEIVED – ARE MADE EVIDENT.

8.

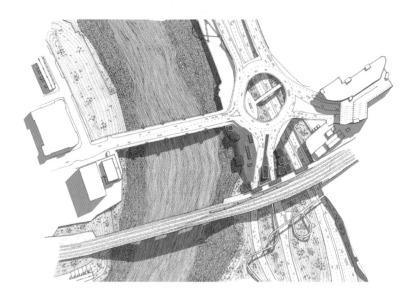

FASHION SCHOOL WOVEN INTO PIER/IS
AND PREVIOUSLY UNDESIRABLE CONTEXT
OF ROAD, WALKWAY, UNDERPASS AND
BRIDGE NETWORK.

PEN & INK WASH

ORIGINAL : 500 x 500 mm

Ceri Williams statemodern@hotmail.com

LONG SECTION CUT THROUGH ACCESS
WALKWAYS IN 'TRENCH'

PEN & INK WASH WITH PHOTOSHOP

ORIGINAL : 2400 x 700mm

Ceri Williams statemodern@hotmail.com

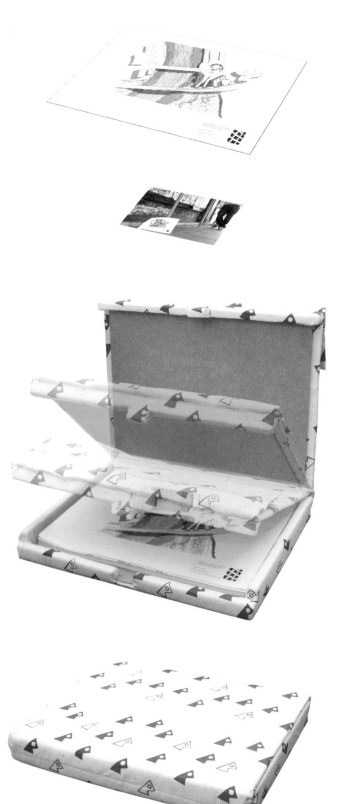

# Richard M. Wright

## Strategy

The primary intention of this contribution is to demonstrate how the two strands of my working life, namely academia and practice, co-exist and cross-fertilize each other. There is also a more specific intention of demonstrating how two separate portfolios of work, albeit linked by an underpinning ethos, can be placed within the same context. This generates what is termed a 'hybrid portfolio'.

The first consideration for the author undertaking the production of a portfolio of design work is how it will be viewed. The portfolio consists of storyboards of work and as such requires structure and possibly a sense of graphical continuity. The structure tends to be relatively easy to resolve, particularly in the context of architectural portfolios, as projects generally follow a linear path in terms of their development and the resolution to design and presentation. If a sense of graphical continuity is not present in the work but is required, then the production of a portfolio becomes more difficult – it is no longer simply the collation and presentation of work, but instead becomes a design problem. This is true of the hybrid portfolio illustrated, where there are two very different projects with no physical or graphical sense of connection.

The answer to the design problem for the hybrid portfolio was to take inspiration from the Barbican Centre in London. This is a very complex set of buildings, combining residential accommodation with a theatre and exhibition spaces. One solution for allowing easy navigation of the site was to paint colour-coded lines on the walkways which visitors are asked to follow for particular destinations within the complex. This strategy has been translated and used within the hybrid portfolio, to allow the viewer to garner a sense of commonality and continuity between the two projects and understand at what points they converge and diverge.

Once this strategy of connecting lines had been decided upon it then became a very enjoyable process of working out their trajectories, style, organization, and, most importantly, the set of common rules they should follow, in terms of the way they interconnect and connect images.

## Production

The page layouts and the graphics were constructed in Adobe Illustrator. The graphics were then exported as EPS files and the complete content was rebuilt in QuarkXPress. The rationale behind this approach was that Quark is one of the better page-layout applications for printed output, but Adobe Illustrator is most suitable for the initial relatively complex graphics. The use of multiple programs and indeed the combining of media to achieve a desired outcome is a common practice in my design studio, be it academic or practice. Many of the images illustrated are the result of the combining of media, for example CAD, painting, photography, drawing, and several graphics programs.

## Advice

The production of this hybrid portfolio was a challenge, but also an opportunity to reframe and reconsider my work. The production of a portfolio of work is always an opportunity to re-evaluate the work to be collated, and should be seen as an opportunity to observe, reassess, and possibly reconstitute the work. However, portfolios should always be constructed for a purpose, and that purpose requires careful consideration and should be viewed as a design exercise in itself, with inspiration being sought from the broadest possible sources. A portfolio is a mini design project, and it should be treated as such.

**case study**

The hybrid portfolio, defined in this instance as a collection of student constructs and built forms by different authors, each linked to the other by a common design process extolling a particular design sensibility.

The projects and method of depiction illustrated here attempt to establish physical connections and proximities between works that were never intended to co-exist in a single portfolio. The real connection between them is an underlying design ethos, brought about by the practice and teaching activities of the author of this chapter.

The idea of 'portfolio' in this instance is clearly challenged in its traditional sense, the work could and was collated as separate physical portfolios for very particular reasons, for example, entry into the Royal Institute of British Architects (RIBA) President's Medals Student Awards, planning permission and the construction of a building. The value of this portfolio is as an explanation of a design process, and how a common underpinning ethos can generate very different outputs suitable for many applications, yet still remain tangible and valid in each iteration of activity. Beyond this it attempts to give insight into how ideas can be used as commodities, freely translating from an academic to a practice environment, to somewhere in between.

01

There are primarily two portfolios of work illustrated, the student project 'Crash – House for J. G. Ballard' and the practice project The Gill House, they are displayed concurrently. The rationale is to demonstrate their commonality and the point at which they begin to diverge. The illustrations also attempt to show how ideas and actions offshoot into other projects and activities. The genesis for each project is the same, the exploration of site; the notion of site being expanded to anything that has a connection or relationship to the project.

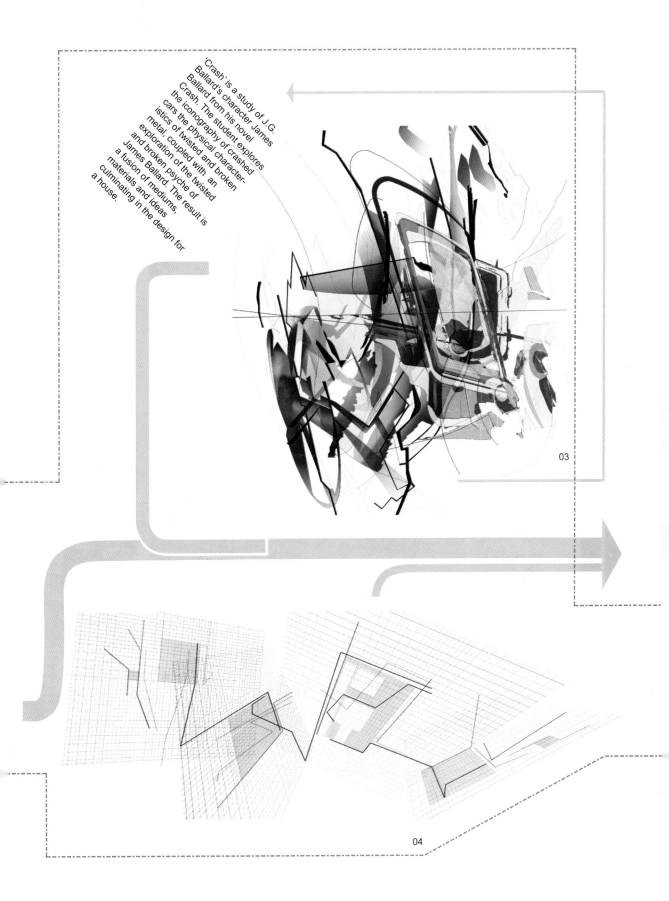

'Crash' is a study of J. G. Ballard's character James Ballard from his novel Crash. The student explores the iconography of crashed cars the physical character-istics of twisted and broken metal, coupled with an exploration of the twisted and broken psyche of James Ballard. The result is a fusion of mediums, materials and ideas culminating in the design for a house.

03

04

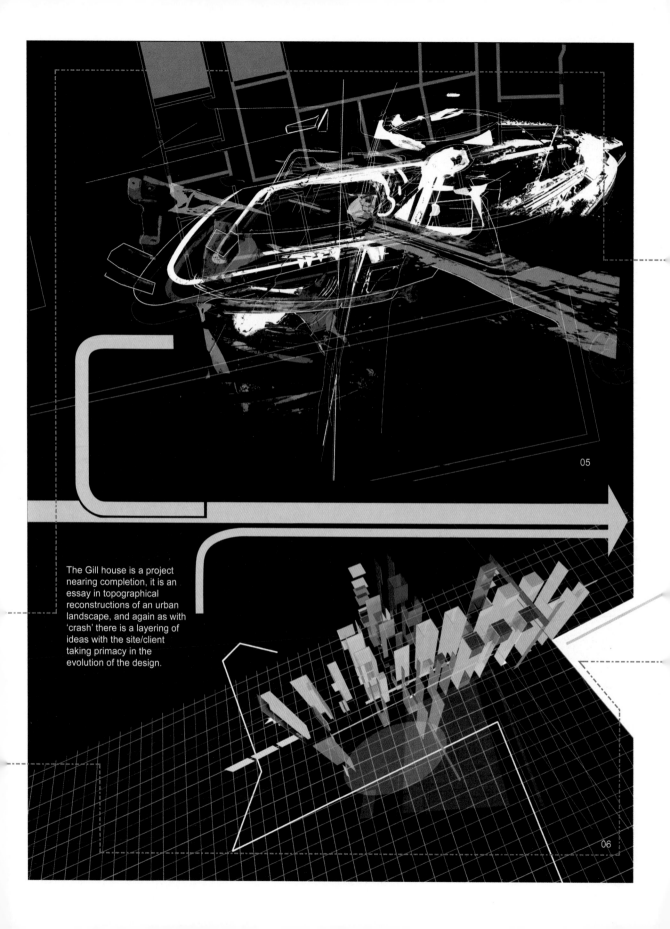

The Gill house is a project nearing completion, it is an essay in topographical reconstructions of an urban landscape, and again as with 'crash' there is a layering of ideas with the site/client taking primacy in the evolution of the design.

05

06

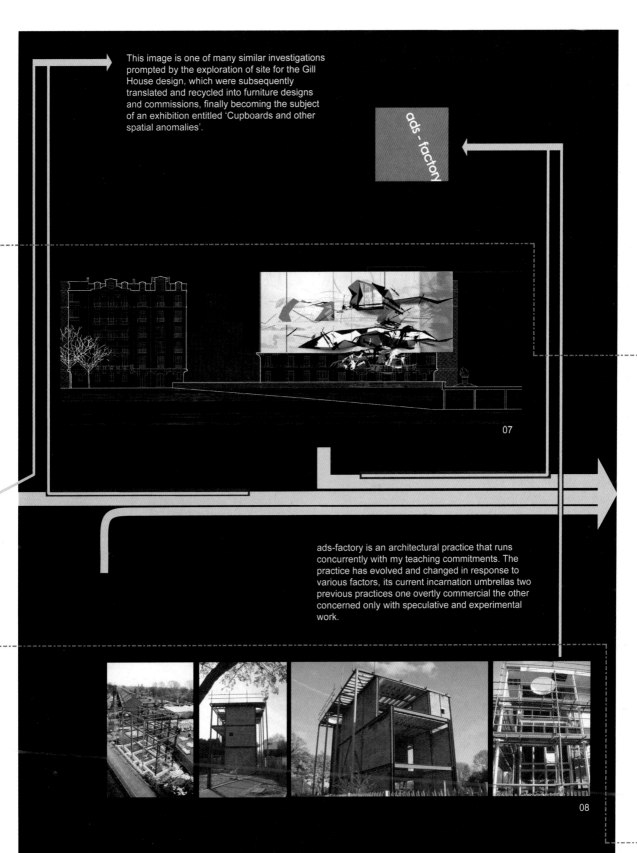

This image is one of many similar investigations prompted by the exploration of site for the Gill House design, which were subsequently translated and recycled into furniture designs and commissions, finally becoming the subject of an exhibition entitled 'Cupboards and other spatial anomalies'.

ads-factory

07

ads-factory is an architectural practice that runs concurrently with my teaching commitments. The practice has evolved and changed in response to various factors, its current incarnation umbrellas two previous practices one overtly commercial the other concerned only with speculative and experimental work.

08

09

Collaged rendered views demonstrating the projected evolution of the interior of the building as the character/client Ballard adds crash artifacts and memorabilia to his home.

12

List of Illustrations

01 installation, reconstruction of a crashed car, photograph. Mark King
02 encoding drawing of site recordings. ads-factory
03 translation drawing from installation. Mark King
04 translation drawing from site recordings. ads-factory
05 drawing depicting initial attempts to fuse site with generated
   architectonic language. Mark King
06 interpretive drawing of generated architectonic language, fusing
   two streams of form generation with site parameters. ads-factory
07 elevation of proposed façade. Mark King
08 photographs showing progression of construction. ads-factory
09 interior rendered view. Mark King
10 interior rendered view. Mark King
11 exterior view. ads-factory
12 exterior view. ads-factory


Credits

ads-factory.co.uk
Principals - Richard M Wright, Peter E Wright
Associates - Barbara M H Griffin, Saleem Al-Mennan

Student Project
Mark King, RIBA President's Medal entry 2008 recipient of the IGuzzini
Travelling Award.
Design tutors Richard M Wright, Saleem Al-Mennan.
Lincoln School of Architecture

# 2
# Plan It, Select It

## Plan It, Select It

Planning should be a familiar and well-practised task. A plan can be as simple as making a list or mapping out a course of action. The importance of planning for a portfolio is simple and straightforward: it must identify the main issues which need to be addressed, and in what order. Planning assures an orderly, predictable, reliable, simple, flexible system of stages in which to develop and refine the portfolio. The stages help to organize the planning process in a streamlined and structured manner. There is an implicit rationale about how the stages will affect the preparation of the portfolio and hence how they will bring about the desired effect – usually getting a job or appointment. The stages can be separate, but they often merge and flow into one another.

The process of moving an idea from the internal realm to a concrete, external, observable realm can be expressed in the universal terms:

1. Understand the problem.
2. Make a plan.
3. Carry out the plan.
4. Look back on your work and consider the implications for future work.

This simple outline shows planning as a field of discovery, revealing to yourself your own thinking process, and helping you learn from experience and reflection. The process of planning is learning to think, gaining confidence, letting ideas come out of the work, being receptive to leads, outcomes, and developments.

Most successful portfolios spend the majority of their time in the analysis phase. Here are two major questions that need answering before you do anything else.

- Who is the audience for the portfolio?
- What are the aims and effects on the audience which you hope to achieve with the portfolio?

The planning stage has the benefit of suggesting a concept or idea for a portfolio that covers the breadth as well as the depth of your knowledge, abilities, and interests. The starting point is always the same: analysis and definition of the nature and purpose of the portfolio – in other words, establishing enough information about your aims and the overall requirements of your audience to allow the feasibility of the portfolio to be assessed. By following your plan carefully you will ensure the portfolio will be finished on time and within budget. Whether you are making your first or your twentieth portfolio, good planning will ensure a style of portfolio appropriate to its audience, using appropriate materials and ideas.

## 2.1  Understanding Yourself

Before starting on the preparation of your portfolio, you must know what you are aiming for. We must not dive straight in with no real clear idea of what we are trying to say or do. In order to honestly demonstrate who you are and how you think (the prime purpose of your portfolio), you must have good insight into your values, interests, temperament, and motivations. When you know what you enjoy and what motivates you, you can produce a portfolio that speaks for itself without clutter or over-elaboration.

### Consider the following questions:
- Is there something that you are really good at that you love to do?
- What theme, quality, or characteristic describes your work up to this point in time?
- What kind of work would you like to do?
- Is there a particular niche or market that you have already identified?
- Do you plan to apply to graduate school?
- Do you want to find an apprenticeship?

## 2.2 Identifying Your Audience

You may have already determined specific work you'd like to do and therefore have specific ideas about your intended audience and the effect you want your portfolio to have on them. Yours will be what we refer to as a **targeted** portfolio. But perhaps you have more than one specific aim. Or perhaps you have made a conscious decision to opt for the flexibility of a generalist as opposed to the narrow focus of a specialist. In this case you will make a **generic** portfolio. There is no absolute division between a targeted and a generic portfolio.

In either case – targeted or generic – you must define a set of assumptions about the audience to be addressed. These assumptions will require understanding your audience and its conventions:

- What do you want to say that is new?
- What do you hope the audience will feel after they've heard and seen it?
- Whose attention do you want and why do you want it?
- How will you convey your message?

The portfolio must match the qualities that prospective employers, readers, and reviewers are looking for. Remember that they will make an immediate judgement. Beyond 'seeing' what is in the portfolio, they will be persuaded by intangibles such as skill, sophistication, instinct, taste, and who you are as an individual.

Outline the purpose and goal of your design in a programme or statement of intention. Summarize your aims. State your theme, preferably in a single sentence. Even if you can only articulate your intentions in general terms go ahead and write them down. It is in the nature of the design process that you will develop and refine your aims as the project progresses. State problems clearly and simply. Remember the word 'focus'.

## 2.3 Conserving Work

Your growing body of original work must be protected from dust, weather, pets, and loss. In practical terms 'conservation' suggests organizing a storage and retrieval system that is responsive and functional for your particular needs. Most damage is done to items while they are being handled (e.g. during inspection or transport from one location to another, especially over very short distances). Determining the storage and retrieval system that will work best for you involves the following considerations:

- frequency of use
- method of use
- ease of access to item
- means of preservation

### Duplication and back-up

First things first, whether your work is digital, print, or 3D, always make copies of originals. Err on the side of caution, and duplicate everything. Otherwise let cost help you determine your hierarchy of importance. Consider the things you couldn't live without if they were damaged or lost. The following are standard methods for duplicating your work:

- photocopy
- photography
- digital photography
- digital scan

Multiple copies of original work should be made as soon as possible. Files can be lost, paper can be torn, models can disintegrate, servers can fail. Keep in mind that nothing is permanent and CDs have a shelf life of 10 years.

If you have digital files set up a routine for making back-ups on a regular basis. In this way, you can restore any item that is lost or damaged and you will not spend time and money to reproduce the work all over again.

## Image file types

TIFF (Tagged Images File Format) files generally retain more information and JPEG (Joint Photographers Experts Group) files are usually smaller and easier to save and convert. Generally speaking, TIFF files give better printing results, while JPG files are good for displaying on the screen. Keep in mind that exceptional quality is essential for all of your images for inclusion in your design portfolio.

Make sure to get crisp edges on the image and high dpi (dots per inch). You should aim for a standard format (e.g. letter size in the USA or A4 in Europe) and a high resolution image of minimum 300 dpi. Consequently, when an image is scanned in at 300 dpi, there are 90,000 dots or bits of electronic data (300 x 300) in every square inch.

Remember that with computer-aided design and computer animation files you must preserve the original qualities (lines, value of tones, and colours).

## Photographic files

The professional quality of your reproduction is essential to match the excellence of the work itself. It may be necessary to use a commercial reprographic laboratory which can reproduce your work using colour laser printers and colour image scanning.

## 3D objects

Models (both formal and exploratory) and sketches have a very limited shelf life, so chances are you have already made a photographic record. If you haven't done so now would be the best time.

Taking slides, photographs, or digital images of your 3D objects is the most challenging and time-consuming part of the documentation. If you can, use your school laboratory and borrow professional lighting. For the best results, shoot indoors using clamp-on reflectors and tungsten-balanced photo flood bulbs. Shooting outdoors with natural light is also possible, but the results are more difficult to control. Try to capture the best views by emphasizing the strengths of your design – for example, take close-up shots of interesting details.

## Organizing for access and meaning

Think broad categories. There are many ways to select and order your work. Categories might include process documents, hand sketches, illustrations, computer stuff, diagnostics, and analytics. The following broad categories might be used to separate your work:

- chronology
- size
- medium
- subject

CD-ROMs and Universal Serial Bus (USB) mini storage technology dramatically expand information storage capability. The CD-ROM is a stable and reliable tool for information storage and delivery. Most importantly, it can become a flexible archive which can be updated and tailored according to specific project requirements. You can archive your work on CD-R (recordable) simply by having your slides scanned onto a CD-RW (rewritable), or having your work digitally photographed and directly saved into an image file.

### Labelling and indexing

File names have to be specific. It's a good idea to make an index of your work so you can find it once you've put it in storage. A standard collection record form is an ideal way of keeping track of your work. Decide on the most suitable method of recording the different types of work you have and prepare a layout for the form accordingly. When you have developed a satisfactory form, have sufficient copies printed/ duplicated.

### Cross-referencing

The card catalogue might be undervalued. List categories that might be useful to you. For example:

- analytical investigations
- expertise in technical areas
- aesthetic issues
- computer competency
- conceptual thinking

When you are finished, review the categories you have created and make any refinements necessary to keep your work accessible. Always keep categories broad enough for quick storage and retrieval. During this process of duplication, categorization, indexing, and storage you will find a stack of pieces with no real portfolio potential. You will also find duplicates of drawings, sketches, old research materials and documents you feel are mostly invalidated. Eliminate them or assign them to a storage category of their own: nostalgia.

## 2.4 Selecting Work: Building the Theme for the Portfolio

We simply cannot reveal everything about ourselves to a particular audience; it is impossible. We must edit the information to make it germane to the occasion. Just as a textbook author must pick and choose information so that a reader gets the point without getting overwhelmed or confused, so must we pick and choose information to make our points in the portfolio. Begin by clustering related objects to express your ideas or build your theme.

The objective of this important stage is the preliminary selection of work for inclusion in your portfolio. The value of the planning stage is the instant articulation of a model or prototype that offers one a chance to see oneself and one's work in the context of one's own intellectual and imaginative development. Big ideas first, details later. Avoid getting lost in the details.

Look for dominant characteristics which may serve as unifying concepts for the design, layout, and sequencing of your portfolio. Refer to your programme or statement of intention to keep you focused on the selection of work. You should separate out work that reveals your thought processes and your individual creative approach. Remember that your portfolio is always more than a collection of separate pieces and develop an underlying structure and narrative thread in a visual and intuitive way. The portfolio is an important tool for self-presentation because it reveals in a graphical way both the direction and depth of your experience. It offers hard evidence of problem solving and presents documentation of a unique story. Commit yourself to making your ideas immediately comprehensible.

## Yes/No/Maybe

This exercise is a fast and effective way of making an initial sort of your work for inclusion in your portfolio. The technique is structured to enhance your objectivity while reducing emotional attachment to your work. The key is speed and instinct.

Ask a friend to stand at a distance from you and hold up one piece of your work at a time. You should assume the objectivity of a critical reviewer and respond to the sight of each piece with 'Yes', 'No', or 'Maybe':

- 'Yes' is confined to work that makes a strong statement; work that requires no explanation or apology; work that is immediately engaging and visually appealing. If you say 'Yes' the piece goes in the keeper file.
- 'No' includes any work that isn't self-explanatory, and/or work that reveals your weakness, not your strengths. If you say 'No' the piece goes directly back to storage.
- 'Maybe' includes work that is desirable perhaps, but not essential. The 'Maybe' pile also includes work that requires remodelling/reworking to make it portfolio-ready. Work in the 'Maybe' pile will be subjected to a second round in the Yes/No/Maybe elimination process after you have completed the first run-through.

In this exercise you want to separate out work that is most revealing of your thought processes and your individual creative approach.

## 2.5 The Crit Wall

Perhaps 20 or 30 samples of work have emerged from Yes/No/Maybe. Remembering that your portfolio is always more than a collection of separate pieces you can now develop the underlying structure and narrative thread of your portfolio in a visual and intuitive way. It may be easier to perform this operation by spreading your work on a table or the floor. Either way, begin by looking for natural ways to cluster or group the pieces. Look for dominant characteristics which may serve as unifying concepts for the design, layout, and sequencing of your portfolio.

Brainstorming is a fast and versatile technique which may be used at this or any other stage of the planning, design, and production process to generate a great variety of ideas and information. Ask a friend or teacher (ideally someone with relevant knowledge or experience) to participate. No previous experience of brainstorming is necessary. Work to the following rules:

- State the problem clearly and simply.
- Encourage a relaxed, creative atmosphere.
- Decide on a time limit which is not too long, 30–60 minutes.
- Generate as many ideas as possible within the time period: the more ideas there are, the more chance there is of finding some that are really useful.
- Do not criticize or analyse ideas for practicality: responses must be spontaneous and uninhibited.
- Feel free to combine or build on ideas.

Decide on a method of recording ideas (for example, blackboard, large roll of paper, or separate cards). A variety of techniques (interaction nets, bubble diagrams, flow charts) can be used for displaying spatial or other relationships between elements within a design problem. Instead of having to draw out a full-fledged version and get lost in the details, thumbnails are widely used as an intermediate step for generating the actual plan layout of your portfolio and for visualizing all the factors and variables that have a bearing on the design process.

Now take a few – four or five – of the best thumbnails and make some larger sketches from them. Make them the size of a note card or a full sheet of paper. But limit yourself to just a few. Don't try this with all of your thumbnails, just the ones that show promise. Explore your thoughts in a larger format, roughing out some more detail in order to get a feel for the intended groupings, and their relationship to your conceptual scheme. Save the details for the next two steps in Design It, Produce It.

## 2.6 Case Studies

The process of portfolio planning can differ substantially in complexity and language, formality, adaptability, aim, and application. However, the underlying principle is the same: it should be an orderly procedure of thoroughness and completeness, with each systematically determined piece geared towards the creative tendencies of the designer.

The process of refining an idea is often not linear, and involves negotiation and feedback at each stage. Planning stages are prone to modification as they are implemented. This is an inherent and necessary characteristic. In the work of Dimitris Argyros, Jan Leenknegt, Rebecca Luther, Ana Maria Reis de Goes Monteiro, Jennifer Silbert, and Daniel J. Wolfe we can find points of connection and comparison in the highly individualistic process of developing the aims and means of solving a design problem.  As will become clear in the following case studies there is a lively diversity of approaches to planning.

**CASE STUDY 1**
**Dimitris Argyros's** sketchbook is conceived as a self-documenting field for intuitive and rational inquiry. The unstructured environment and self-documenting dynamic processes allow physical exploration and design. The sketchbook does not assume a finished product within a certain time frame or, necessarily, an audience. Argyros's method is designed to give traction to the immediate with the least disruption to continuation. The sketchbook is the spirit and physics of architecture reenacted on a smaller scale.

**CASE STUDY 2**
**Jan Leenknegt** borrows the structure of a Michel Sorkin's manifesto to organize a portfolio of coursework and project documents. Leenknegt allows the thematic organization of ideas to acquire new and promising connections, creating new possibilities.

**CASE STUDY 3**
**Rebecca Luther** conceptualizes her portfolio as a collection of short stories (autobiographical essays). Her conscious decision to design for three different media formats produces a portfolio that is flexible enough to adapt to different audiences.

**CASE STUDY 4**
**Ana Maria Reis de Goes Monteiro** considers the potential of systematic documentation at intervals throughout a project. Conceptual breaks are bridged by individual colours drawn from a unified palette of colours. Besides their practical navigational function, the colours are clear, simple, forceful communications of the mood and heart of the work.

**CASE STUDY 5**
**Jennifer Silbert's** diagrammatic page layouts are an extension of her investigations into the physics and tectonics of a design problem. Diagnostics, statistics, predictions, and formulae are organized in a rational grid.

**CASE STUDY 6**
**Daniel J. Wolfe** conceptualizes his portfolio as a structure of linkages and relationships that extend, ultimately, to an audience which then contributes to the further development and evolution of the work. The original structure is geometric, rational, but endlessly reformed (free-formed) as needed.

# Dimitris Argyros

## Strategy

The concept of the sketchbook as the portfolio is an alternative to the clinical, glossy printed CAD pages that tend to be the basis of a student's project portfolio. Rather than dressing up a project towards the end of the year in the computer with fancy text, graphics, and logos, the student can spend time pushing the design by regularly documenting and processing the work produced inside and outside an A3 book of white cartridge paper using a selection of computer and traditional hand-production techniques of printing/cutting/sticking/folding/tearing. The idea is that if something is cut, glued, and labelled, chances are you won't go back to it to 'refine' it. More importantly, the sketchbook becomes a physical extension of the designer and integrates design and documentation within one collective process that demands all the senses, not just the visual.

## The sketchbook thus serves three roles:

- Documentation and processing of site information, programmatic research, and larger pieces of work produced outside the sketchbook.
- Design development through various media – sketching, text, pictorial collages, fold-out models, cut-outs and further processing of the documentation of models and drawings.
- Intimate storytelling of the concepts, design parameters, and design stages for any external critiques.

## Production

A basic layout can be set at the beginning of the year, although this can be adjusted to varying sizes and intuitive decisions. This makes the selection and editing process easy, intuitive, and, most importantly, fun. All the work made inside and outside the sketchbook should be quickly and methodically documented and labelled. Intuition and sensual interaction are essential. The visual sense is key to a designer's process of thought and a viewer's understanding, so collages, diagrams, sketches, drawings, photographs, and photograms are important tools. However, the other senses are equally important. By engaging the portfolio through turning, unfolding, and touching the pages both designer and viewer can explore and understand the project more deeply. Pages can be rubbed with flowers or engraved with the soil of the site; and the sounds or rhythmic properties of a building or a place may be described.

Getting the balance between a personal design diary and a clinical design description is key to the success of the portfolio, and this comes about gradually. Some pages may be important as a design concept whereas others may be important as explanation. When the portfolio needs to tell a story to others, pages that are less successful or unimportant can simply be clipped and not shown. Others that are key to the idea can be temporarily marked with a sticky tab. On other occasions, A0 size drawings can be folded into the book. The choices are endless.

## Advice

- Trust the concept of the project and not the graphics that help only to dress it up.
- Experiment with any means available. The design process is not intended for the benefit of the viewer or even the critique but for the benefit of the design concept and the development of the project.
- Text and labels should be small and neatly stuck down. Let the images and the design process speak for themselves.
- Be neat. Letting go of the computer does not mean having a dirty portfolio.
- If you are rushed and don't have time to add text and labels, simply tag the pages and come back to them later.
- Find the balance between being free and intuitive and also organized and methodical.
- Remember that the portfolio is a reflection of yourself, so make sure you express yourself and your project to others the way you want to.

**case study**

## Sketchbook as Portfolio

The sketchbook as a portfolio is an alternative means to the clinical, glossy CAD portfolios that tend to inform most of project design development and presentation. Rather than dressing up the project and portfolio towards the end of the year, the sketchbook allows one to use hand-production, traditional techniques that concentrate on pushing the design throughout the educational year. The portfolio takes on three roles:

### Sketchbook as Archiving

As an archive diary, the book, with its informal layout can be a quick and easy process of holding research and documenting design work. A layout can be set by the designer at the beginning of the academic year, but can be flexible enough to adjust to the size of the work or the intuition of the designer at the time. Printed or hand-text can be used to label the work, important both for designing and explaining to a viewer.

Archiving references and precedent

Sketching/drawing ideas

### Sketchbook as Designing

As a design tool, the sketchbook becomes an extension of the designer. The thick cartridge pages can either be sketched and drawn on or be cut/folded and pasted as collages, relief pull-outs and even models. These traditional techniques can be hybridised with more conventional computer aided design tools to add a more personal 'touch' to the designers' project process and presentation.

Collages and montages

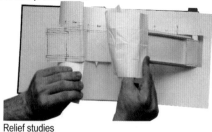

Relief studies

### Sketchbook as Narrating

As a story-reading to an outsider, the sketchbook creates a personal relation between the narrator and the listener. The reader engages with the book through a personal interaction, by turning/folding/unsealing/pulling the pages. With its manageable size and the ease to clip certain pages and highlighting others, it also allows the narrator to set up a pace that can be quick or slow, depending on the listener.

Leaflets and pages can be handed out to viewers

Narrating can involve many viewers

Luxor By Horse Portfolio (A3 size)

An eco-friendly transport system using Luxor's existing horses and carriages attempts to alleviate Luxor Central of its urban congestion and tackle the problem of land deprivation and poor horse care. A transport Union is also proposed.

As a means of protecting Luxor's limited available soil, the Union, situated at the boundary of the city and the farming strip, takes the form of a network of dense accommodation towers, connected via monorails and undulating landscapes.

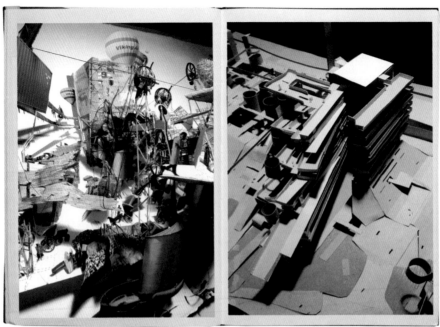

The horse-accommodation towers attempt to re-create a natural environment for the horses, by providing a cool environment for sleeping and eating. Their construction is a hybrid on new and vernacular technologies built by the locals.

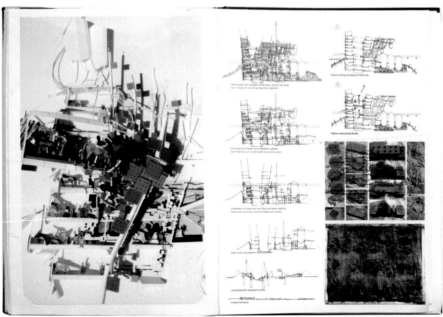

A sustainable manure-adobe brick links the process of food and waste, raw materials and equine inhabitation acting as an insulating dry façade and as a sustainable responsive greening façade, without the use of additional water or soil.

Final presentation perspective model

Final presentation sectional model

# Jan Leenknegt

**1.**

**What (if any) sources did you study or adapt in producing your own portfolio?**

I based my portfolio on a text by Michael Sorkin, *Eleven Tasks for Urban Design* (2004). I like the manifesto-like clarity of the book because it sharply contrasts with the open-ended discussions I had experienced during the three semesters of the Urban Design programme. On the first introductory page of my portfolio, I explain this reference and introduce the reader to the framework and organization of the rest of the document as follows:

> In March 2002, Andrea Kahn and Margaret Crawford organized a conference called 'Urban Design: Practices, Pedagogies, Premises'. While I was packing and preparing to start a Masters in Urban Design at Columbia University, directors of eight North American urban design programs got together and evaluated three decades of urban design education. At that conference, Michael Sorkin presented his 'Eleven Tasks for Urban Design', a fresh and funky manifesto that outlines how urban design can make a difference, 'in the vacated crack between archiitecture and planning'. I decided to use Sorkin's Eleven Tasks as a framework for this portfolio. Each page after this one represents one of the Eleven Tasks. Sorkin's title and manifesto text on top, my studio work and texts in the middle, and additional course work on the bottom. So the work I produced in the three design studios is not represented chronologically, but thematically.

Eleven pages, one for every task, and an introduction page, which makes 12 tabloid pages, exactly meeting the strict SOM (Skidmore, Owings & Merrill) Foundation requirement.

**2.**

**How did your production timetable and budget evolve?**

I made the portfolio in between graduation and the SOM Foundation deadline, little more than a week later. After having been selected as a Columbia representative for the SOM Foundation competition, my school granted me $300 for the production of my portfolio (as prescribed by the competition guidelines). I used this budget to make a real manifesto board for every task.

**3.**

**How long did it take you to produce your portfolio?**

Four days, full time.

**4.**

**Did you seek help during the production of your portfolio?**

Apart from a friend who helped me craft the binder, there was no one else involved in making the portfolio.

**5.**

**Did you have to submit a statement of purpose for the SOM Foundation application? Was the design of your portfolio related to your statement?**

I did not have to submit a statement of purpose. Since the award is funding for travel, however, SOM Foundation contestants have to submit a travel proposal, on an extra (13th) sheet. The travel proposal is not directly related to the portfolio (not part of the Eleven Tasks), still it follows the same graphic language (font style, paging, spacing). On the bottom of the 'Secure the Edge' page of the portfolio, I refer explicitly to the travel proposal.

**6.**

**How did your previous portfolios differ from the one you submitted to the SOM Foundation?**

For the first time, I organized my work thematically and did not present it in a merely chronological way. The basic requirement for the SOM portfolio – only to present work from the Masters course in urban design – allowed me to choose a tight conceptual frame, namely Sorkin's Eleven Tasks. It is important to note that, by reworking my studio projects and course assignments in a thematical way, I looked at my own work through different glasses. Trying to find (dis)continuities, similarities, and themes throughout a whole year of intensive production, I was able to take some distance from what I had had right in front of my eyes continuously during the previous 12 months. Working on previous (more conventional) portfolios ended up being just another reproduction of the projects I had been presenting several times already.

**7.**

**Do you adapt your portfolio for different purposes or do you present yourself to every potential client in the same way, saying: 'This is me'?**

So far, I have never restyled portfolios dating from different 'periods of work' to one single portfolio. The different periods of work are shown in the different styles they were originally presented in.

**case study**

*"There is simply no substitute for the physical spaces of public assembly. Increasingly imperiled by commercialization, electronification, criminality, and neglect, both the idea and the forms of gathering are a central subject for the imagination of urban design. Public space is the lever by which urban design works on the city, by which the subtle relations of public and private are nourished. A fixation on the media of production of these spaces has overcome any passion for their quality, even as a Nielseneque resignation stupidly celebrates any gathering, however it is induced. Urban design must keep Giants' Stadium from annihilating Washington Square even as it seeks all the alternatives inbetween. The Internet is great but it ain't the Piazza Navona: free association and chance encounter still demand the meeting of bodies in space. Embodiment is the condition of accident and accident is a motor of democracy."*

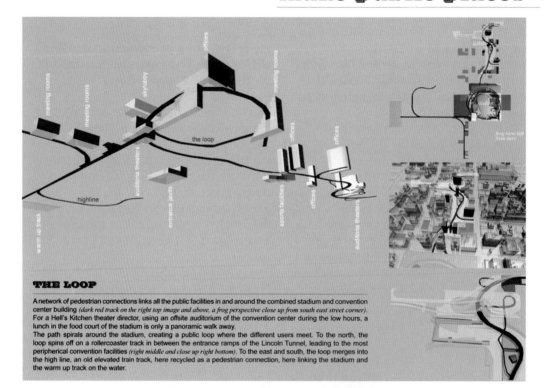

## THE LOOP

A network of pedestrian connections links all the public facilities in and around the combined stadium and convention center building *(dark red track on the right top image and above, a frog perspective close up from south east street corner)*. For a Hell's Kitchen theater director, using an offsite auditorium of the convention center during the low hours, a lunch in the food court of the stadium is only a panoramic walk away.

The path spirals around the stadium, creating a public loop where the different users meet. To the north, the loop spins off on a rollercoaster track in between the entrance ramps of the Lincoln Tunnel, leading to the most peripheral convention facilities *(right middle and close up right bottom)*. To the east and south, the loop merges into the high line, an old elevated train track, here recycled as a pedestrian connection, here linking the stadium and the warm up track on the water.

## AND 2 PLATFORMS

On the street level, two platforms perform as people collectors, especially useful for major stadium events. One platform *(dark red)*, slightly below street level, functions as a distribution slab between the parking levels, the train platforms of Penn Station, and a ceremonial space to the east. From the second platform *(orange)*, slightly above street level, elevators take the visitors to the stadium, to the convention spaces, to the loop.

The project for Bangkok proposes vast detention areas around emerging subcenters. Water management and agriculture are definately the primary role of those areas, but still they can be crossed and visited in multiple directions. Fruit tree plantations alternate with recreational areas. We considered Parco Agricolo Sud Milano *(images to the right)* as a good example.

A similar strategy for Saw Mill Landfill Park. Rather than being a main attraction in the New York metropolitan area, this park should keep the wild, adventurous and mute character of the closed landfills. *(see "defend privacy" for design proposals addressing this "limited accessibility"*

[public space and recombinant urbanism]
### BAGHDAD
a study of patterns of public space throughout Baghdad's history

[digital filmmaking]
### THE HIGH LINE
A three minute documentary about a 1.8 mile long abandoned elevated train infrastructure between downtown and midtown Manhattan. Currently under debate whether to destroy or to transform to an elevated walkway.

*"It's time for a radical shift toward human locomotion in cities. The automobile is not simply a doomed technology in its current form; it has proved fundamentally inimical to urban density. Enforcing the hydra of attenuation and congestion, the car usurps the spaces of production and health, of circulation and enjoyment, of greenery, of safety. Fitted to the bodies of cities which could never have anticipated it, the car is a disaster in town. We cannot again repeat the mistake of retrofitting the city with a technology that doesn't love it, with railway cutting or freeways. Cars must lose their priority, yielding both to the absolute privilege of pedestrians and to something else as well, something that cannot yet be described, to a skein of movement each city contours to itself. This may well involve various forms of mechanical (or biological) technology but urban design – in considering the matter – should reject the mentality of available choices and formulate rational bases for fresh desires. If we can't even describe the characteristics of superb urban transport (invisible? silent? small? leisurely? mobile in three axes? friendly?), this is because we haven't taken the trouble to really imagine it."*

# 03
# elaborate movement

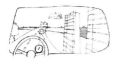    

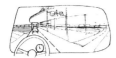    

## CROSSING THE DETENTION LANDSCAPE

With the clay excavated from the detention ponds, certain areas which are or will be served directly by subway, canals and through roads are elevated. Those plateaus will attract dense development. The diagram to the far left shows the plateaus (black) together with the 500m radius around both orange and blue subway line stops.

Dotted with boat taxi stops, subway stops and highway accesses, each plateau has a different accessibility profile and will attract a specific type of development. An example to the left (legend is the same as the map of "be sure rooms have views").

The drawings show sequences of how the project area can be crossed by car, train and foot, each time focusing on another element of the detention landscape.

## TRAVEL TO NEW JERSEY

Whenever Robert Sullivan has a free afternoon, he travels from his Manhattan office to the jungle behind the Palissades and climbs Snake Hill, the only natural hill in the Meadowlands. Marc Ribot knows there are buses and trains to his hills of New Jersey, but "somehow he just can't go". Up to today, the Headquarters of the Meadowlands Commission (and thus the starting point of the majority of the walking trails) are only accessible by car. By linking the perimeter of the park to the New Jersey coastline lightrail and by making intermodal train-boat-walkway connections, I believe that the bits and pieces of the landfill park, cut apart by the crossing highways and freight train tracks, could achieve a first unity. Besides linking the closed landfills to the rest of the world.

[future for manhattan's westside waterfront]
## AFTER OLYMPICS

The subways on 8th avenue are way too far away to induce the desired activity on the Westside waterfront. Subway extensions are expensive. Our mobility framework focuses on an intensified ferry system (a circumnavigational vaporetto with several crosshudson services) closely interwoven with a crosstown lightrail system (vision42 deluxe) and pedestrian connections.

# Rebecca Luther

## Strategy

My portfolio is conceived as a thoughtful collection of short stories. Individually, each story recounts a project's temporal and physical context, and the specific architectural process that was undertaken at that time. Collectively, the stories come together to form a larger narrative spanning the past 15 years. This collective narrative reveals common threads from one project to the next, and has been a valuable tool for self-reflection.

Etymologically speaking, a portfolio is a carrying of individual leaflets (Italian portafoglio: from Latin portare, to carry, and folium, leaf or sheet). In my own portfolio design process, I make a clear distinction between the individual project story, or leaflet, and the collection, or packaging of these leaflets. While the individual stories are snapshots in time, and their contents and organization remain relatively consistent from one iteration to the next, the collection is in constant flux. I often rethink the selection, the re-presentation, and the intended collective message of these stories after new inspirations, for new audiences, and as my own personal interests continue to evolve.

In order to best address multiple target audiences (from wide-eyed new architecture students, to busy clients, to myself as self-critic), I required the current iteration of my portfolio to perform triple-duty: 1) it had to be an enticing 'sampler' of foldable leaflets containing my individual project stories; 2) it had to be clear and well-proportioned when viewed digitally; and 3) it had to function as a portable bound collection of past work and ongoing thoughts, receiving bookmarks, news clippings, digital media, and notes.

## Production

Due to the multi-tasking nature of this particular portfolio, I required that it be quickly and efficiently infilled, edited, printed, and produced. It had to fold, expand, flip, and tuck. Like a well-worn travel journal, it had to sit comfortably in the hands. Although my original drawings, models, and built works are often quite large, my portfolio is quite small. It captures the essence of the work on the boardroom wall, and moves it into the palm of the hand. This allows me to collect a body of work into a portable, reproducible medium that appears personal, accessible, and understandable in a single viewing.

Given my self-imposed requirement of addressing multiple audiences, the current iteration of my portfolio is produced in three alternate formats: 1) the marketing mailer; 2) the laptop view; and 3) the journal. All formats began with well-documented (scanned and photographed) images, carefully categorized and digitally filed. The project story, or spread layout, is the heart of my portfolio. Although its basic structure always remains fairly consistent, it had to be edited to work for all three formats: I use a combination of hand-drawn cartoon sketches and publishing software in my portfolio spread design.

**Advice**
I have several rules of portfolio design that my students commit to memory. These include tried and tested quips such as 'Use multiple scales to create micro/macro readings' and 'Create movement across the spread'. However, I have found that it is my final rule that is the most useful: 'All rules are made to be broken, so trust your eyes, and follow your heart'.

**case study**

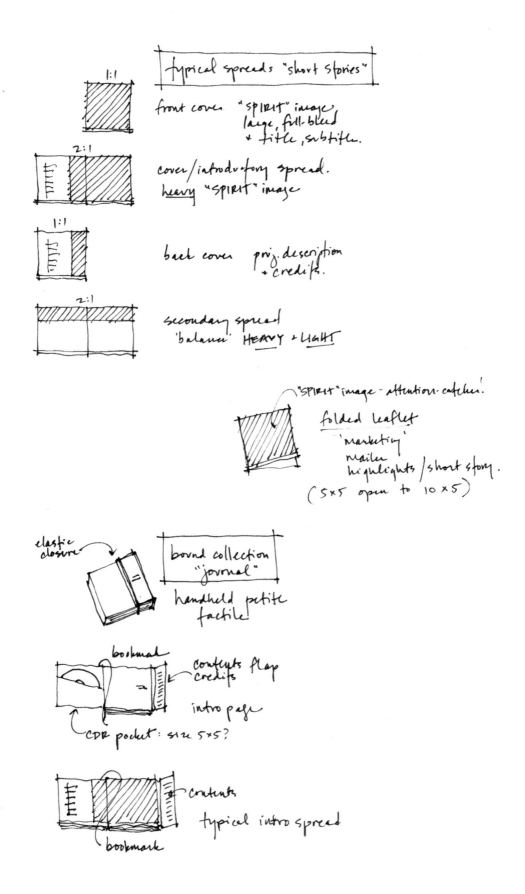

**typical spreads "short stories"**

1:1

front cover "SPIRIT" image,
large, full-bleed
+ title, subtitle.

2:1

cover/introductory spread.
_heavy_ "SPIRIT" image

1:1

back cover  proj. description
+ credits.

2:1

secondary spread
'balance' HEAVY + LIGHT

"SPIRIT" image - attention-catcher!

folded leaflet
'marketing'
mailer
highlights / short story.
( 5×5 open to 10×5 )

elastic
closure

**bound collection "journal"**

handheld petite
tactile

bookmark

contents flap
credits

intro page

CDR pocket: size 5×5?

bookmark

contents
typical intro spread

rebecca luther
# portfolio as storyteller

## one story; three views

The challenge was to design a double-sided spread that could capture the story of an individual project for three different audience types / collective viewing formats. Folium size, proportion, graphic layout and information placement had to function well for all three portfolio formats.

## 1. the "marketing" mailer

An individual 10"w x 5"h double-sided project story spread, printed on card-stock and folded in half to form a 5" square leaflet. The introductory spread becomes the cover, with the full-bleed "spirit" image on the front and the project description on the back. The inside contains the secondary spreads. Used as a handout, or mailed in a 5" square translucent envelope.

## 2. the laptop view

Digital pdf file containing a collection of individual project spreads in series. The 2:1 proportion of the spreads allows for computer display viewing clear of software toolbars.

## 3. the journal

A 5"w x 5"h x 1"d booklet, perfect-bound and secured with a fold-over clasp and elastic strap. Inspired by pocket-sized travel journals, it has a pagemarker and pockets (in this case for digital media and news clippings) secured within its chip-board covers. The inside of the clasp contains the contents list.

Facing page:
Excerpts from my sketchbook.

rebecca luther
# a project story, detailed view

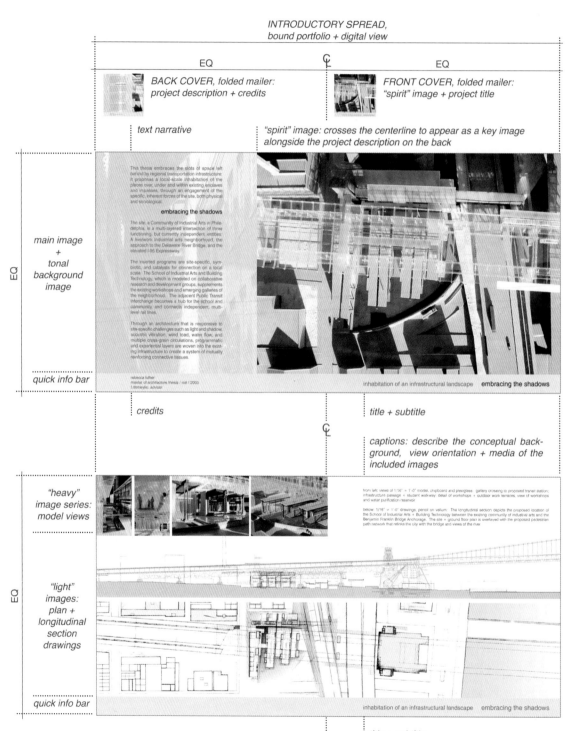

INTRODUCTORY SPREAD,
*bound portfolio + digital view*

EQ      C̷L      EQ

*BACK COVER, folded mailer:*
*project description + credits*

*FRONT COVER, folded mailer:*
*"spirit" image + project title*

*text narrative*

*"spirit" image: crosses the centerline to appear as a key image*
*alongside the project description on the back*

*main image*
*+*
*tonal*
*background*
*image*

EQ

*quick info bar*

*credits*

*title + subtitle*

C̷L

*captions: describe the conceptual back-*
*ground, view orientation + media of the*
*included images*

*"heavy"*
*image series:*
*model views*

EQ

*"light"*
*images:*
*plan +*
*longitudinal*
*section*
*drawings*

*quick info bar*

*title + subtitle*

*center fold/bind line*

C̷L

## introductory spread

Each project story begins with an introductory spread that also serves as the cover in the folded leaflet version. A large, full-bleed image that captures the spirit of the project is paired with a desaturated background image and the project title, credits and description.

## secondary spreads

Projects have from 1 to 5 secondary spreads. These spreads often begin with analysis of the physical, cultural and sociological site of the project. They also include selected sketches and study models, and project documentation in the form of conventional plan, section and elevation drawings, perspective views, and photographs of the built work.

## movement and rhythm

Each spread is intended to have a dynamic balance of "heavy" + "light" images that lend the story movement and rhythm. This rhythm of "heavy" + "light" is repeated at the larger collective scale when the portfolio spreads are viewed in series, as at right. The rhythm provides for dynamic viewing of the portfolio in any of its three formats: folded (and unfolded) leaflet, digital series of spreads, or flippable bound booklet.

Right: Series of spreads, each with a thumbnail view of folded leaflet cover.
Facing page: A closer look at typical introductory + secondary spread layouts.

## Ana Maria Reis de Goes Monteiro

### Strategy

Making a portfolio is tied to the systematization of work developed by those in the profession. However, the systematization of the documentation of a work in progress by architecture students can also be seen as a portfolio inasmuch as it shows the process of a project. The process whereby students work on a portfolio shows their needs and potential which then gives the instructor an invaluable tool for individual evaluation. At the same time it helps the students in the learning process.

When working on such a project students tend to develop techniques of reflection, criticism, creativity, and independence. It is necessary to reflect in order to organize one's thoughts, thus encouraging critical thinking. The need to demonstrate ideas stimulates creativity. The fact of being an individual requires developing one's own independence. The development of such abilities contributes in a decisive way towards forming one's own identity.

### Production

Various methods can be used in developing and producing a portfolio. In the case of organizing the documentation process of an architectural project, at the same time showing the theoretical research that guided its conceptualization, students make several kinds of investigations. Expressed by means of croquis, photographs, and by actual and virtual models, the material is organized into what we call a project album. In the course of study several albums are prepared, which make the following possible: the evaluation of the project assumptions and assumed methodologies; a decision about the guiding principles to be followed to best express proposals graphically; agreement on a method to organize the ideas and themes. In this process maquettes and traditional design techniques are used synchronically, by hand and on the computer.

The preparation of the summary in an album is important since it presupposes the understanding of the process as a whole, that is to say, of the intended objectives. The inside pages of the album should relate to one another and fit into a general structure. The structure of the project album presupposes the right selection of graphic figures.

It seems to us that the organization of the project album is one of the key points, not only in the way that through it one can question the objectives and initial assumptions of the project, but also by the fact that the portfolio ought to express clearly the process of the project. The portfolio is composed of graphic pieces, photographs, electronic maquettes, and it also has explanatory comments. The preparation of the comments has often proved more work than the graphics. The written part has been revised innumerable times in a constant effort to upgrade.

**Advice**
The preparation of the project album / portfolio is a unique moment for students for self-evaluation and reflection about their own work. The work should express clearly the progress of the project and contain its concept and project references. Well-written text is important, but often images, croquis and diagrams speak for themselves. Therefore, it is important to know how to use various kinds of media and computational programs. It is a personal expression. For this reason, besides the method and the organization, it is necessary that it be creative and that it reflect the personality of the project author.

case study

**Sumário**

Sumário

Área de estudo      Pessoas a quem se destina o projeto      Estratégias de projeto

The documentation created during an architecture student's project can be organized in the form of a project album or portfolio. Its goal is documentary while it registers the project process, but it is also a form of presentation of a finished work.

    The structure of the portfolio and the quality of presentation are crucial in order that the proposed objectives and the project process be understood perfectly. For the project process of the student to be clear it is necessary that some of the stages be mentioned: for example, the understanding of the location where the project is placed, and the understanding of who will be living in that specific place and what their activities will be. It is equally important that the student reveal his or her project strategies.

    In the case in question, a colour was designated for each one of the stages. This can be seen in the colour of the words of the summary. So for each one of the phases there is one item that corresponds, and for each item there is a matching colour. The colour attempts to establish a connection between the pages and also between them and the general structure. In this way each chapter begins with the corresponding colour and with a graphic summary of its content.

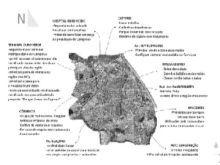

The image above left expresses the graphic synthesis of the area of study. It was designed after inspections were made.

The map shows the course of existing waterways, the urban network and urban facilities such as the public hospital and the bus terminal – key locations of the region.

The image below presents the project stategies: urban connections, bicycle paths, parks along streams, emphasizing the centrality brought about by the urban facilities.

**Territorialização**
Campinas

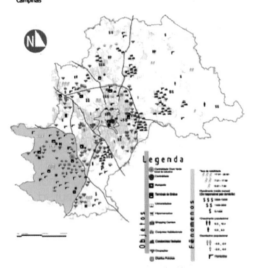

The portfolio should include a written part which is conceptually consistent. The data referring to population should come in the form of text, maps, tables and graphs. However, the experience of the student along with his or her sensitivity can create expressive images which often succeed in highlighting social and cultural diversity with greater clarity.

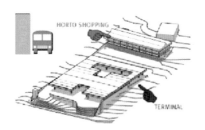

HORTO SHOPPING

TERMINAL

GRADES

TALUDE

COMÉRCIO
INFORMAL

MUROS

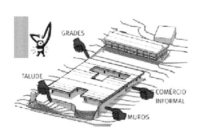

PEDESTRES

PEDESTRES

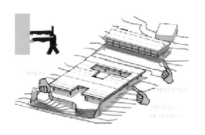

# Jennifer Silbert

### Strategy

This portfolio showcases a year's worth of research and 3 graduate projects in a short-format folio book, 9" x 16". The vertical orientation of the large-scale originals dictated the vertically oriented pages and was a natural choice for the grouping. The tectonics of the object was very important to me: therefore, the book is heavy and smooth, with elegant dimensions that are enjoyable to handle. By design, the portfolio is impactful and informative, using single-page vignettes to tell a larger project story. Over time, this portfolio has become like a diary or art piece that I look back on for inspiration. It is precious but well-worn.

This portfolio was only the fourth I had ever attempted, and was by far the most successful in strategy and execution. The first two were for school applications; the third catalogued my first-year graduate studies; and this final one was my application for the SOM Foundation award, showcasing 3 research-based architectural projects. My technique was refined to include only the best images from each project (process sketches, drawings, model photographs, and site photographs), with extremely concentrated explanations. The small amount of text comes from the original presentation drawings, so the journey is mainly a visual one. As school projects these are both theoretical and practical, and in all 3 cases I carefully chose images that were complex and appealing, presenting the final project while clearly focusing on the process.

Because it is a school portfolio, my inspiration for the work and the book came from my professors – Robert Mangurian and Mary-Ann Ray, who use smart text to enhance images, and words as images themselves (their book, *Wrapper* (2000), has always inspired me, particularly their stamp signature in my personal copy); Cecil Balmond's focus on algorithmic design helped me develop a complexity in drawings and models that was able to speak for itself, without explanatory text; and Turner Brooks's unique, boisterous, and extremely playful style allowed me to break out of the grid and be bold. These lessons are in the portfolio – the work and the layout – where it was important to be clear, precise, confident, and to have fun.

### Production

The maximum size and number of pages was dictated by the submission guidelines for the SOM Foundation award. Most of the images in the portfolio were originally produced as vertically oriented posters, so a vertical portfolio was the most natural choice. There is little or no explanation on most of the pages, and the design process is simply shown in chronological order, so the viewer reads the project as it was created. I chose to showcase 2 projects, on 15 pages, with one additional supporting project. This means that each main project has 5 pages to be fully explained. Each page stands alone, and also contributes to an overall understanding.

All the photos (model photos / site photos) were taken using a digital camera. Hand sketches were scanned and the book layout was done primarily on a PC desktop computer, using QuarkXPress and Adobe Illustrator. All of the drawings for the Serpentine Pavillion project (shown) were created using AutoCAD drawings translated to Adobe Illustrator. The final files were printed from Illustrator. Also included are hand-made sketches, collage models, and mixed media drawings. The book is hand bound using a perfect bind that is easy (for an amateur) and neat.

**Advice**

When actually producing this portfolio, I followed one rule rigorously: include only those images and texts of the very top quality. I value a concise, powerful statement over a barrage of words and images, and I am extremely cautious of over-stimulation clouding the work. My main advice is to be objective in editing, which is a difficult process (particularly when dealing with such personal work it is hard, but very important, to leave mediocre images out). At the most basic level, choose quality over quantity, and focus on a meaningful understanding of each project.

case study

## BASELINE GRID WITH 3 VARIATIONS

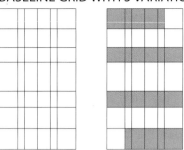

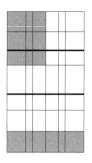

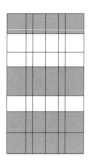

The baseline grid is set up as a reference to give underlying structure to each page. The variations within this grid are endless, and once the grid is set up, I am prone to breaking it. Each page, therefore, ends up with its own unique layout diagram based on the grid system.

For photograph pages, such as the one on the right, weight was an important factor in the overall layout.

## GRID DIAGRAM

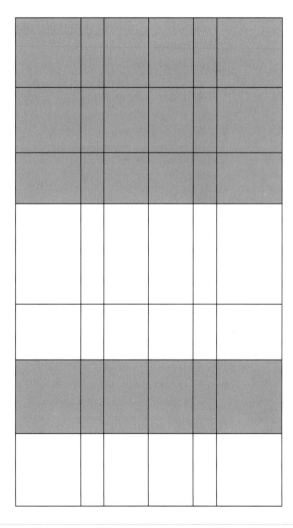

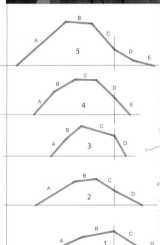

**Imagination**
January 2003 – Photo-Collage of Pavillion

CUT LINE 9" x 16":
A standard size 11" x 17" page is trimmed down to make a more elegant silhouette. Pages are printed on a laser printer and hand trimmed.

Images tell the story of the installation. There is no descriptive text.

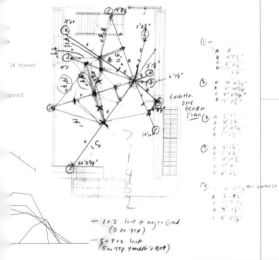

16 thread

proof

The fabrication process is also explained through sketch and working drawings, without additional text.

The initial concept sketch juxtaposed with the final installation gives a clear understanding of the starting and finish points for the project. The page layout, juxtapositions, and intentional ommisions of overt explanation, seek to challenge the viewer creatively and analytically. Without requiring it, one can spend alot of time on each page.

Below the final image is a very concise explanation of the project.

## Realization

April 2003 – Construction of the Serpentine Pavillion on the Roof of the Art + Architecture Building – Full-Scale Test of Algorithmic Space-Making

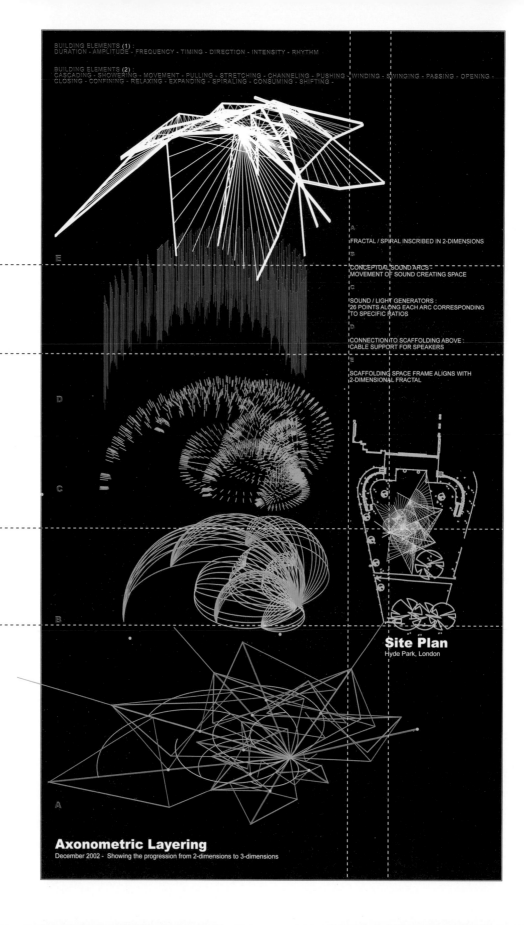

BUILDING ELEMENTS (1) :
DURATION - AMPLITUDE - FREQUENCY - TIMING - DIRECTION - INTENSITY - RHYTHM

BUILDING ELEMENTS (2) :
CASCADING - SHOWERING - MOVEMENT - PULLING - STRETCHING - CHANNELING - PUSHING - WINDING - SWINGING - PASSING - OPENING -
CLOSING - CONFINING - RELAXING - EXPANDING - SPIRALING - CONSUMING - SHIFTING -

A
FRACTAL / SPIRAL INSCRIBED IN 2-DIMENSIONS

B
CONCEPTUAL SOUND ARCS :
MOVEMENT OF SOUND CREATING SPACE

C
SOUND / LIGHT GENERATORS :
26 POINTS ALONG EACH ARC CORRESPONDING
TO SPECIFIC RATIOS

D
CONNECTION TO SCAFFOLDING ABOVE :
CABLE SUPPORT FOR SPEAKERS

E
SCAFFOLDING SPACE FRAME ALIGNS WITH
2-DIMENSIONAL FRACTAL

**Site Plan**
Hyde Park, London

**Axonometric Layering**
December 2002 - Showing the progression from 2-dimensions to 3-dimensions

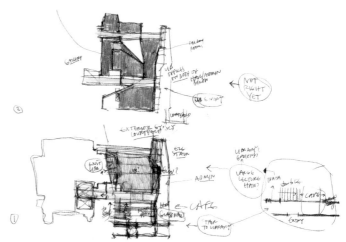

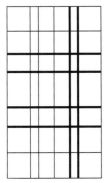

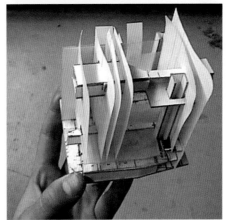

The page LEFT is a progression in design process and time, from a flat drawing at the bottom of the page, to a 3D modeled structure derived from that same flat drawing. The layout of the page, with the exploded process, emphasizes this concept. The small plan drawing on the right side is the necessary context to an otherwise totally abstract drawing sequence.

The page layout is subtle, using the 1/4 and 1/3 vertical grid lines to break out of a rigid structure, creating overlaps.

Because there are no weighty images, the entire page relies on the "reading" of the image sequence. This typology is considered differently than an image-heavy page.

The RIGHT emphasizes the working process, which I strive to include in all projects. The process can give unique insight into a cohesive final design.

Each page strives to tell a complete story, as well as to support the overall understanding of a project.

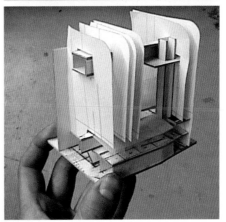

## Daniel J. Wolfe

**1.**
**What are your inspirations and influences?**
I would have to say a large portion of my work is influenced by graphic design campaigns that focus on product design. This type of marketing is focused on several concepts that are closely related to goals I have for my own portfolio. While the graphic compositions are often powerful and compelling the designers maintain a distinct hierarchy within the advertising: product, company, and then auxiliary graphical elements. I feel this can be contrasted with projects, architect, and graphical elements – an organizational structure that I feel is essential to successful architectural portfolios.

**2.**
**Do you keep many portfolios? What distinguishes one from another?**
I do not keep more than one portfolio. I find that with every project I reach a new level of subjectivity and understanding. I am constantly redefining what I understand as architecture. As my sensibilities mature I develop a strong distaste for my past works, finding it difficult to use as a means of self-promotion.

**3.**
**Is your portfolio designed as a summation of your current preoccupations or is it designed as a continuum of your work as a whole?**
My work is always reactive, and the content of my portfolio is dictated by the setting in which it is anticipated to perform. Before I create a new portfolio I require a catalyst. A situation must present itself that requires the development of a new portfolio. As a result, my portfolios are performance-driven designs. Project selection is the product of performative evaluation based upon constraints set forth by its intended goal.

**4.**
**Do you use your portfolio as an inventory or archive of your work?**
No. As I mentioned above, I seldom enjoy my past works. I often feel that my distaste for the past is what motivates me in the present.

**5.**
**Is your portfolio a stream-of-consciousness, incorporating whatever contributes to your feelings without necessarily having any particular literal meaning in relation to the material?**

No, my portfolios have a monolithic aesthetic, with a clear marketing message. I feel arbitrary graphical elements should be kept to a minimum. I prefer clean compositions with concise systems of organization that focus on the presentation of the project.

**6.**
**Is your portfolio primarily design-driven or is it project-driven?**
**Is it primarily image-based or is it primarily text-based?**

My portfolios are project driven utilizing a combination of images and text. The text is supplemental and subservient to the images at all times. The projects in my portfolio have taken endless amounts of time to develop; a reader could not possibly understand the premise of the project by viewing the design solution. As such I reserve this text to provide the reader with a back story to help understand the premise for the design.

**7.**
**How do you gauge the effectiveness of your portfolio?**

My portfolios are always generated with a specific goal in mind; application for a professional position or school admission, or an attempt to acquire a commission for a project. I measure success relative to that initial goal. Conversely, subjectivity will often reveal that the portfolio as a composition may not be at fault. At points in my career I have found myself to be in situations that required a distinctly different portfolio typology to be successful. The lack of success was not attributed to the graphical composition; however, it was due to a lack of experience in a particular area.

case study

# Daniel J. Wolfe

//A four dimensional diagrammatic concept;

## Initial Configuration

Rigidity of the initial diagram represents the initial conception of the idea of the portfolio. Variation is a result of intuition and feedback inherent to the morphological nature of the design process.

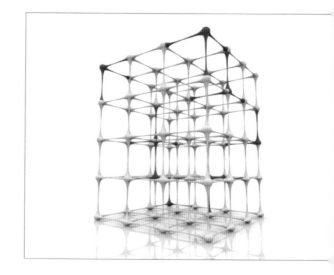

## Network Augmentation

As the iterative process experiences several cycles an increasingly sophisticated aesthetic emerges. Aesthetic and performative attributes from the collection of projects evolve in parallel to the performance of the overall aesthetic.

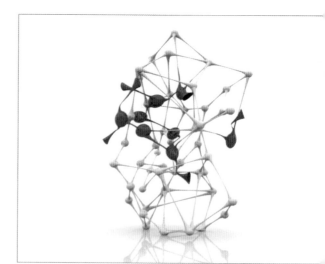

## Micro Scale

The nodes of the network represent individual projects, as the projects performance evolves it infuses the design process with intelligence. This intelligence opportunistic evolves the balance of the remaining projects.

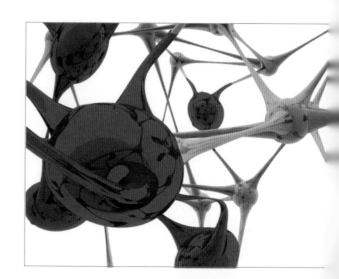

# Micro Scale Process Morphology

//Primary Design Phase;

( 1 ) Initial State, Project Selection; The
preliminary design process yields information
for qualification of projects for inclusion.

( 2 ) Project Augmentation;  Projects are adapted
to achieve improved aesthetic and performative
attributes.

( 3 ) Compositional Experimentation; Intuition
creates opportunistic variations on the original
rigid portfolio configuration.

( 4 ) Aesthetic + Performative Evaluation;
Subjectivity; This is a performance test and
feed back loop.  Upon evaluation the designer
returns to stage one.

Network Reconfiguration

# Selected Work

//Projects + Pages;

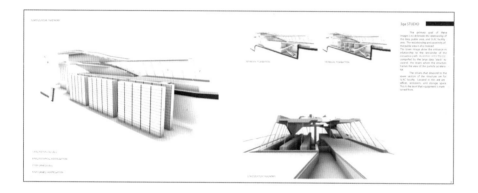

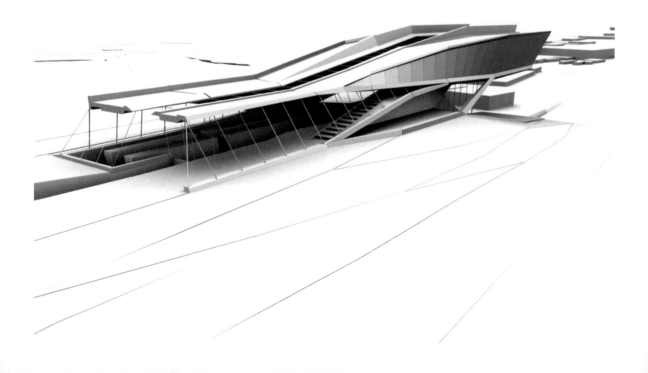

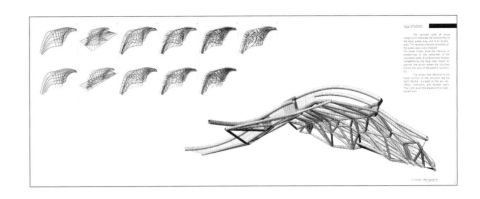

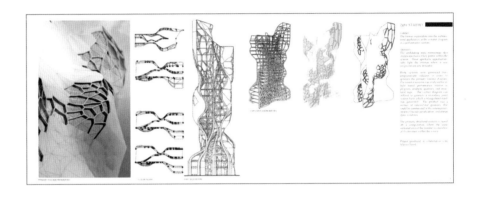

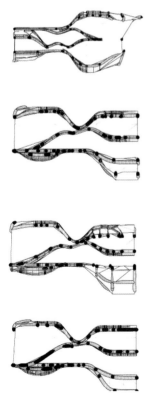

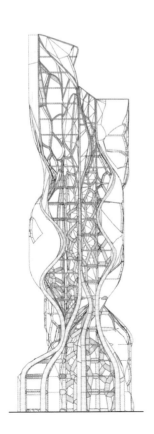

**3**

# Design It, Produce It

## Design It, Produce It

After the planning process and
selection of work that may provide
the best supporting evidence for
a concept of the portfolio, the next
phase is design. We use portfolios
to make our ideas apparent. The
perception / reception of ideas is
sometimes difficult since they are
usually presented indirectly and are
therefore subject to interpretation, but
they are vital in the content and form
of portfolios. Generally the portfolio
is a flexible thing, evolving as new
information and ideas are drawn
together into broader contexts, and
relational patterns. However, there are
some basic structural requirements
to consider. These guidelines are
flexible – they must be so in a process
which emphasizes dialogue. The main
thing is to arrive at a unified visual
statement that explains, visually, not
only what you are doing, but why, and
what it means in the context in which
you are working.

## 3.1 Thumbnails and Mock-ups (Dummies)

After a preliminary selection of work supporting the concept of the portfolio, you may have some idea about the sequence and theme for how you will organize information.

Your first design decision involves the physical size and proportion of the portfolio page (and the screen page). From there it is easy to continue to other aspects in a confident manner. There are two elementary devices for investigating structural possibilities for the layout: thumbnails and mock-ups (or dummies). Both methods generate quick glimpses of the important issues of shape, placement, sequence of pages, and links within the shared space of the single narrative – book or digital. Both allow a freedom to experiment because of ease of feedback, assessment, adaptation, variation, revision, etc. This technique of quick, pre-verbal, instinctive composition enhances confidence in personal sensibilities and character (i.e. originality of style).

Some designers are able to use thumbnails to rough out a good book sequence, especially of digital pages. Mock-ups or book dummies, on the other hand, go to the physical roots of a portfolio. The physical impact of the mock-up as an appeal to the senses is something shared with architecture's volume, forms, and surfaces. The dummy can test for shape, colour, composition, proportion, paper sizes and weights, materials, and binding. You have to concentrate, be quick, be patient, and trust your instincts. The strength of the dummy is that large issues – primary shapes, proportions, structure, continuity, materiality, movement, colours, and relationships – can be resolved before the more intricate details are refined and polished. Use any content and draw with big markers and crayons to make quick, plan-view sketches in which you can analyse proportion.These sketches are for analysis only. Don't treat them as drafting. Rely on your intuitive response to make quick decisions about the exact sequence, size, feel of the book, and its character as a visual whole – not only within each page, but through the progression of pages.

## How to make a dummy

Now you will build a dummy – a dimensional model of your portfolio. Make sure that everything you learned in the steps where you surveyed portfolio samples and materials and decided on a style is reflected in this model. Go back and look at what changes you made, what contrary directions were taken. Check to see if it still makes sense.

One of the criteria for a mature design is to attain the greatest effect possible from the seeming least means. This economy would, of necessity, have to include physical effort as well as the amount of material or the number of elements, or more.

Think about which of the primary senses will best link momentary experience to the archive's experience in our memory. Remember that distinct materials provide a variety of sensual experiences and add joy to living. In other words, you have to satisfy your eye, and feel it in your gut.

What associative, experiential impact will the portfolio have beyond specific information provided? The net effect of your portfolio is always more than a collection of images.

Now stack 4 or 5 sheets of paper in half, staple at the fold and rough out scale-versions of each page. Using grey-scale markers, coloured markers, or torn paper, make quick, very rough sketches to simulate art and text. You can sketch directly onto the dummy pages or make quick sketches on tracing paper which can then be cut and taped in place and easily repositioned. Don't get caught up too early in detail. Solve the big spatial problems first, then integrate the small forms into the appropriate space. Work out the details in your final piece.

## 3.2 From General to Specific

This is the point where you start recreating the ideas (sequence, pace, emphasis) developed in sketches and dummies into a print or digital form.

### Organize it on paper

The prime purpose of your portfolio is communication. To be understood, information in any form must be organized and direct; even with complicated subjects, information should be presented in an accessible way. Your portfolio must be prepared so it communicates clearly, simply, completely and eloquently.

Finding the right format, size and layout will be a little more complicated than you imagine if it is to make its impact in the way you want it to. Your concept of your portfolio must be clear and unambiguous to communicate your ideas and images in graphic form. How to be different and eye-catching and, at the same time, get the message across is your challenge. It isn't simply a matter of selecting binder, slide pages and page sleeves, and then grouping the images in a logical progression – it must show some kind of consistency, point of view and style. Furthermore, if your portfolio is to be remembered it can relay one principle idea or perhaps two things – three or more and the message will be lost.

Style is a tool, it's the thing you use to hit the target. Think about the colours you want to use and what those colours mean. Think about the imagery that supports your focus, the pace that attracts your audience, the words that communicate to them. Think about the cultural references and landmarks that establish a common frame of reference between you and your audience. Think about the language of materials you want to use and what those materials mean. Think about the forms that support your focus, that will communicate your concept, that will attract your audience.

Never try for 'interesting' arrangements of the parts of your portfolio. The work itself is interesting enough. If the work is not of interest, perhaps the design is weak. No fanciful arrangement of work will make a design stronger if the concept is weak to begin with.

Style should be a result, not a goal. To create a style to legitimize an attitude is to kill the need of creative intellect to search for solutions. Style must emerge and not be imposed. Style must be pertinent.

### Screen-based portfolios

Everyone wants to design 'cool' websites but if visitors to your website can't figure out how to use it in a minute or so, they will leave, or they will be ill disposed towards you, whatever your design capability and technical competency. Similarly, remember that audio layers must support – not distract from – the prime message. Just like every other design element, just because you can add sound does not mean that you should.

Just as with a print portfolio, your audience must be your central concern. From content and page design to designing for ease of navigation and for users with disabilities, you must remain focused on how to connect with your website's visitors. They must be able to:

- Find what they're after quickly.
- Browse quickly and access information in a logical manner.

With tens of millions of websites currently competing for attention, design for usability is the subject of intense commercial interest. Research into what works and what doesn't work in interactive web media has produced a number of books and web sites about web usability, page design, content design, site design, and intranet design. Jakob Nielsen has created a website about usability, www.useit.com. In his book *Designing Web Usability: The Practice of Simplicity* he lists four criteria for the foundation of good web design:

**H**    **high-quality content**
**O**    **often updated**
**M**    **minimal download time**
**E**    **ease of use**

However, according to Nielsen you must go beyond the four basics to have a truly stellar site. To move from a HOME design to a HOME RUN design, add three extras:

**R**    **relevant to the user's needs**
**U**    **unique to the on-line medium**
**N**    **net-centric corporate culture**

### Digital structure and schematics

The simplest of all website structures is a linear design versus random access. The homepage leads to the second page. From there you can go back to the homepage or forward to the third page. And on the third page, you have the choice of going back to the second page or forward to the fourth.

You start adding complexities if you add a direct link back to the homepage from any of these pages. Still more complexity is added if the viewer can jump off the second page in 6 different directions: to a photo gallery, a link page, an email, etc. These in turn lead to other pages, and so on. It's easy to see how the complexities of navigation start adding up. The point of this is to have a plan, ensuring that the various paths make sense to your audience, and include an easy way to get back to the homepage on every page. If visitors to your site do not find it easy and obvious to access the parts of the site they're interested in, they just might not bother.

With this in mind, you can scan in the sketches for your portfolio through a scanner or put the artwork under the tracing plastic on a graphics tablet. Some designers work the sketches into a vector-based program so that they don't have to worry about sizes, rotation, and image degradation unlike with a bitmap-oriented program. Authoring packages are designed specifically for subject experts and designers who may have no programming expertise at all, though this can make them somewhat limited in scope.

Digital schematics are called wireframes because of the way they appear to be nothing more than structural lines that can hold later design items. Wireframes define what goes on the page and how the elements should be prioritized relative to each other. They show user movement through the page, but typically do not describe consequences of a user's action. Wireframes can be created in a wide variety of programs and are probably the most popular tool among information architects. They can also be created with specialized wireframing and site prototyping tools.

**Designing an interface**
The interface is the mechanism through which visitors understand and interact with your website. A good interface gives your visitors assurance that they will be able to find the information they need when they need it. You want to give them a sense of control; they are making the choices about where to go and what to see. You can use logos, symbols, icons, menu bars, buttons, etc. to deliver the context. Use flowcharting conventions for the development of navigational aids to each section of your design.

Computer users are accustomed to visual representation of concepts through icons. They understand visual metaphors such as the trash can. When you design interface elements, tailor them to your expected audience. These links will enable visitors to your site to move effortlessly through all the portfolio entries, following up an interesting lead in one entry simply by clicking on a key graphic and going to the linked entry; then perhaps returning to the original item, or following a link to another item. Remember that readers are familiar with certain screen-based icon systems. Do not make them lose confidence by creating a series of new symbols for them to learn.

**Beyond the web: screen-based portfolio layout**
Web-based portfolios offer a fluid and sustainable vehicle for the presentation of your work. Wide-ranging versatility comes, however, with a host of requirements including writing for the web, cross-platform design, response time considerations, multimedia implementation, navigation strategies, search boxes, international considerations, just to name a few. It is essential to stay focused on whether your web design actually accomplishes its goal, which is usually to sell, teach, or entertain.

All of the issues raised above assume that the site visitor is using a computer, a web browser, and a standard screen to view the website. We all know that may no longer be the case. The web can now be viewed on an iPhone, BlackBerry, or miniature laptop, to name a few devices. The rules that used to apply to graphic design are no longer relevant. Many of the rules of web design are now obsolete as well. Some of the recommendations for creating content that will display well on a handheld device seem positively draconian.

The main limitation of a handheld device is the small screen, which may also lack a mechanism for horizontal scrolling. Navigation may be with a stylus, not a mouse. Downloading to the device is likely to be both expensive and slow – the processors are slow, and the memory is limited. A lot of users may therefore choose to turn off in-line image loading. Consider these limitations for your small-screen design layout:

- Design one column layouts and avoid floats.
- Optimize your HTML by using efficient, semantic markup and CSS.
- Minimize the use of decorative images.
- Do not rely on images or plug-ins for navigation.
- Write good alternative text for images.
- Avoid dynamic effects that specifically require a mouse or keyboard for navigating.

There are methods for solving the small-screen riddle which do not involve simply designing highly restricted pages. The best approach is to use Cascading Style Sheets (CSS), which allowing the same content to be displayed differently, depending on the device.

## Web-to-print portfolios

A portfolio is a portfolio regardless of presentation format (medium). The composition of a portfolio – digital or paper – benefits from sensitivity to thematic/visual continuity and conceptual breaks. Scripting, sequencing, eloquence, clarity, brevity, and uncomplicated accessibility all matter regardless of media.

If your work involves web design or other non-print designs you can still put together printed portfolios, and vice versa. Make screen shots of the work or print web pages from your web browser. Since screen resolution may not always produce crisp and clear printouts you may want to include high-resolution printouts of special logos or other graphics you created for on-screen display. Even if the portfolio is designed for web display, start with a high-resolution version and save it at various stages for printed portfolios.

Printed portfolios may be finished by hand using graphic design, illustration, and layout software programs which allow you to manipulate all the elements. Alternatively there are specialized self-publishing companies that will guide you through the process to make your own book as a portfolio. The traditional black-case portfolio should be assembled with duplicates to preserve the originals.

## 3.3 Full-scale Design

After establishing the content and the overall look and feel of the portfolio design you move to full-scale design and resolve all major and minor design details.

The aesthetic principles that apply to all design projects apply to the design of your portfolio whether it is print or digital. Such principles as axis and alignment, balance, repetition, and continuity, can be directly applied to simple, uncomplicated presentations in digital and traditional media. Despite the fact that aesthetic principles and elements of design are repeated so much that they have become canonical, they are only principles and elements. Designers should not think only of principles and theory when they work. Adherence to the ultimately subjective principles of harmony, balance, and symmetry, will count for nothing if it takes precedence over instinct based on experience (sensory information) and reflection (logic).

## Proportion

There is only one principle you need to know – one principle that governs all of the others – and that is proportion. There is a misconception about proportion that it is mathematics and measurements. Proportion is elemental and can be achieved intuitively, visually, and conceptually. Proportion concerns relations such as containing, overlapping, and mutual completion. Proportion is at the basis of visual shape, pattern, content, and dimensional form.

## 3.4 Designing for Reception

Common sense suggests that your audience will react to you and your ideas in exact proportion and temperament to how you approach the audience. You should attempt to achieve a unified visual statement right from the beginning. A portfolio can end up looking like a lot of piles of scrap paper assembled loosely together or it can be a design with real character. The success of yourdesign solution depends a great deal on the grouping of forms.

Consider the way the elements are joined. The joints are part of the design. Be very careful never to allow the spaces between individual planes or groupings of planes to appear like separate spaces. They are all part of the whole. It's not just a matter of flow, it's a matter of unity.

By designing your portfolio like a piece of architecture, you will address the issues of creation and utilization of space. Designing the layout on a page or a sequence of pages, parallels the design of a room and then a sequence of rooms. Page design, like plan and elevation, is a process of devising not only individual rooms but whole systems or environments. It should be flexible/adaptable enough to allow redisplay and regrouping of items.

A well-designed portfolio establishes a narrative that is concerned with the linear piecing together of continuous or disconnected images and events. It requires decisions about how much space and emphasis to give to each successive visual or tactile event in the linear arrangement of frames, thus creating an impression of movement through pages, spreads, and the portfolio as a whole. Remember that specific qualities are determined not by measurement, but by comparison to and their relationship with other qualities of design.

### The layout grid

Grids have been used since Ancient Egyptian times as a method of organizing spatial relationships. Designers use grids as a means of composing and organizing information. In essence grids provide the structural framework for a design. The grid should be flexible and adaptable enough to allow redisplay and regrouping of items.

The portfolio grid develops from image and text requirements, providing the structural framework for the design. The grid is not only the organizing principle of graphic layout, but it is also the underlying theme of 3D design and even of interiors and buildings. The layout grid helps to pre-plan visual pathways and the 'landscape' of the portfolio.

Think of the grid in larger terms. You'll find that you can gain better control of your design if you are aware of the abstract relationship between the axes. It's 3D, there's opposition, there's valance, there's structure.

Structure can also refer to patterns of emotions; to the chronological development of scenes, episodes, and parts; to the development of ideas or images; to organization of stanzas, paragraphs, or other divisions. Structure consists also of the relationships among parts that are usually described in terms of cause and effect, symmetry, balance, proportion, association, position in time, logical development, and grids.

Remember that random arrangements are completely valid as long as the layout is systematic throughout. The portfolio can be cohesive even while containing pages that are different from one another in layout, design etc.

## 3.5 Learning from Others

As with any other skill or topic, you start with examples you like. You will begin to understand the basic principles, analyse proportions and the relevance of the content, and then make your own adaptations. The same goes for visual idiom, grammar, etc. that you think was invented yesterday. It probably wasn't. There is no need to be an 'authority' – only to be experienced and aware. For now, recognizing a successful typography comes through informed and direct observation. By analysing page and text block proportions you will discover the multiple variations of colour, imagery, typography and structure that are involved in viable graphic solutions. Consider the following:

- Does the book or text emphasize a particular visual navigation?
- Does the organization of the book or text give the viewer directions?
- Is the book or text set up in logical sequences?
- Does the book or text provide a smooth flow from cover to cover?
- Is the book or text clearly defined into visual units and groups?

## 3.6 Techniques and Stylistic Effects

If you are going to work in print, you should know about scaling, cropping, bleeds, overlays, and colour/tonal percentage as important functions of enhancing your portfolio. Those graphic detailing techniques can be used to enhance the portfolio design structure which you have now established.

### Scaling

When you want to reduce or enlarge an image or piece of your work to fit a particular space in your portfolio, scaling is the technique to use. There are many ways of scaling and all of them are based on the fact that all dimensions shrink in the same proportion.

The most common approach uses the geometry of the diagonal to help you work out the final size of your scaled work. Perhaps the quickest way is to place a corner of the image in the corner of the layout space it is to occupy and draw a line from the corner of the image through the corner diagonally opposite. A rectangle completed at any point along this line will be in proportion to the rectangle indicated on the image.

Before altering the size of a photograph or any piece of artwork for portfolio purposes you must first determine what size you want it to be: in other words, you must determine its new proportions when enlarged.

### Cropping

Deleting unwanted or distracting areas of an image is called cropping or recomposing. Cropping or trimming an image can make all the difference between its being usable or not. Cropping can change the shape of your piece or it can enable you to zoom into a small area of the image and refocus attention. A pair of L-shaped pieces of cardboard can be used to frame the area of interest, thereby helping you to see what the image will look like when cropped.

### Bleeds

A bleed offers the opportunity to expand the visual boundary beyond the edge of the image after trimming. The continuation of the portfolio image beyond the edge will expand the horizon of the viewer.

### Overlays

An overlay is a transparent or translucent sheet (e.g. mylar or vellum) containing graphic material – such as text, coloured areas, or conceptual sketches – which is placed on illustrative work to be incorporated into it. Overlays can create a stimulating design experience and provoke the reader's imagination.

**Colour/tonal percentage**

Colour is established by blocks of information and text. Colour can be used as a metaphor. Colour and tone (dark/light) can be used as graphic 'detailing' or as a flourish, but – as with all other 'finishing' techniques – it must be used only to reiterate your already established design structure. It must not be used to compensate for a perceived emptiness or lack of excitement. Colour can be introduced in full-colour images (prints or originals); in the use of coloured paper or film (section dividers, for example); or as rubrication (traditionally this is red text). Colour should come directly out of the work in your portfolio.

## 3.7 Copy/Text

The images and/or objects in your portfolio will be accompanied by explanation, although this will not always be in the form of the printed word alone. Now you will begin to involve language, using the very words which will appear on information panels and labels.

How well you prepare your copy is of primary importance. If you can cut your copy to the fewest words possible, of course do so. The most effective portfolios have a singleness of purpose best achieved by brief captions or headlines, not by long compositions. If you can't cut your own copy, get someone to do it for you.

On matters of legibility and visual acuity, you will make a number of empirical decisions. Most importantly the information set out on labels must be standardized to help the viewer. Navigational aids such as page headers or footers, icons, and frames help your portfolio establish a flow pattern.

## 3.8 Typography

Typography is a fascinating discipline in its own right and can be extremely complex. Not only are there hundreds of typefaces in existence, but there are many variations of these typefaces: roman, italic, light, medium, bold, ultra-, or extra bold, plus varying degrees of letter condensation and expansion.

In the spirit of keeping things simple, you could use a universally appealing and versatile typeface, such as Helvetica. With simple modulation a single typeface can be used to great effect. Consider the following issues:

- hierarchy of importance
- the play of point size within a single typeface
- text formatting, such as italics, bold
- position – whether left, centred, right, justified, or forced

### Legibility and readability

Legibility is concerned with the very fine details of typeface design, and in an operational context this usually means the ability to recognize individual letters or words. Readability, however, concerns the optimum arrangement and layout of whole bodies of text. An illegible type, set it how you will, cannot be made readable. But the most legible of types can be made unreadable if it is set to too wide a measure, or in too large or too small a size for a particular purpose.

### Typographical features

Too many typefaces on one page can become distracting and disconnecting (by lacking unity).

Try using no more than 3 fonts per project.

**Remember that too many weights can cause** a reader to be unclear where important elements are on a page. This creates the possibility of the reader missing something significant.

### White space is not blank space

We get used to seeing objects and not the space surrounding them. Yet space is especially important for easy reading. It provides a resting place or breathing room for the readers and makes reading much more comfortable. Considerable marginal space usually indicates luxury or formality (unless limited content is being 'puffed up' to look like more than it is), while limited marginal space indicates economy.

### Leading/line spacing

Spacing between the lines allows readers to follow lines of text without losing their place. Too little space can cause a cramped feeling. It's important to remember that different fonts need different line spacing.

### Line length

Reading many long lines of type causes eye fatigue. Readers are forced to move their heads and eyes more often from one line to the next. The maximum attention of a reader is gained with lines of text under 50–60 characters long.

## 3.9 The Cover: An Interesting Entrance

The cover of a portfolio, like an architectural enclosure, reveals the character of the person or firm who creates it. It is a conceptual and experiential environment for the contents. The cover contributes more than just a literal statement. It is a decisive first impression and you have to be analytical enough to see what message is conveyed. You can be forceful and insistent, direct and tactful with the cover design, but do not underestimate the importance of how it feels when held.

The cover functions at many visual and conceptual levels simultaneously. It is an invitation to the reader conveying the vitality of the contents. In its very practical intention the cover acts as advertising of the contents. It also provides emphasis for significant elements of the portfolio through close attention to the intricacies of the design. This prolongs attention to the practical information.

Consider the following qualities for the cover:

- fabricated from material with character that is pleasant to touch
- made with material suitable for its likely use
- legible, with attractive lettering
- sound, appealing design
- agreeable use of colour
- a case that is neat and durable
- easily opened
- pages should lie flat

### Selection of cover image

The cover is both a package and a billboard for the portfolio. Cover design involves tensions and compromise. It is often difficult to capture images of pages of intellectual content in a single graphic statement. There must be some balance between promoting your architecture philosophy, reflecting the content, and being an effective marketing tool. If the image of the cover is too creative, the prospective reader may not understand what kind of portfolio it is. If the image of the cover is too imitative or conventional, the portfolio may disappear among several look-alikes.

Consider the following requirements for a cover. It must:

- reflect the nature of the work
- prolong visual involvement
- be simple, clear, and direct

**Selection of title**

The purpose of the title is to represent the contents of the portfolio. Bear in mind that your title is an extension of you, your work, and your participation in the profession. The audience you hope to reach must be intrigued and attracted by your title. Finally, it should provide clear, reliable cues for the theme(s) of your work.

The title of your portfolio should:

- be assertive, but restrained
- intrigue and attract
- avoid unnecessary words

## 3.10 Paper

The sense of touch is another way to communicate your design intention to your audience. Thoughtful selection of paper can be used to bring subtleties of texture to your portfolio that strengthen your message. Combinations of paper style can provide endless tactile possibilities for the reader. For example, a smooth, glossy, medium-weight cover stock followed by a rough, light-weight end page can highlight the portfolio work as a tangible approach. Remember that the significant qualities of the paper are determined by their relationship with the other elements of the portfolio, not measurement. There are many factors to consider when selecting paper for your portfolio, but there are five distinct qualities that you should be aware of:

- colour
- weight (particularly if mailing)
- opacity
- surface finish (matt/satin/gloss)
- tactile nature

A swatch book, a stapled set of sample sheets showing all the colours and weights in a particular range, can help you to identify the paper that is right for your portfolio.

## 3.11 Binding

The purpose of the binding is to hold together the leaves of the portfolio, protecting them against normal wear and tear, and allowing the portfolio to be opened easily. There is a conceptual aspect as well, concerning the dialogue between physical context and intellectual content. There are many binding processes, but the two basic types are office and craft bindings.

**Office bindings include:**
- The stitch technique, commonly known as booklet making, which applies staples and stitching along the fold of the pages.
- The wire technique, commonly known as spiral or plastic binding, which uses a continuous spring-shaped piece of plastic to bind the pages together.
- The tape technique, commonly known as thermal or perfect binding, which fuses cloth tape to the document along the left margin, forming a spine.

**Craft styles include:**
- Japanese binding which produces so called pouch books – the pages, folded at the front edge and sewn at the back edge, form pouches.
- Post binding, sometimes known as a transfer binding, which uses a screw and post inserted through a hole in a pile of loose sheets.
- The accordion book, composed of a continuous folded sheet of paper which may be enclosed between two covers; it can either be expanded outward or kept flat.
- The pop-up book, a general term that encompasses various forms of 3D or movable books; at its centre is motion created by turning a page, pulling a tab or turning a wheel.

**Boxes and zippered cases are also popular for portfolios. They include:**
- The lipped clamshell, a one-piece design opening flat to allow easy access to the work inside and providing a full-sized viewing area.
- The tray box, a two-piece design of an overlap box that can be used for presentation or archival storage.
- The overflap folio, a thin folder that has an extended cover flap that folds over and can hold a small number of papers or prints.

## 3.12 The Squint Test

Now evaluate your portfolio composition by using the squint test. This is a remarkably effective and quick way to gauge the impaction of your overall design. The test has the effect of reducing details to large-scale contrasts. It instantly allows you to see the large shapes of your design and evaluate it in terms of 'negative' and 'positive' space. Its power is the power of abstraction because it reduces complexities to their most basic form: counterpoint, rhythmical movement, tension, line, breathing spaces, and focal zones come to the fore and are easy to see.

You will also benefit by asking someone else to look at your work. He/she may notice things you have missed or make inferences that you did not intend. Consider any suggestions and comments carefully. We are often protective of our work, but if we are designing to communicate to an audience we need to design for them. Suggestions won't always be right, but they won't always be wrong either. Viewing your work through another's eyes will give you a new perspective, and often some very good ideas.

Of course, nothing is as valuable as your own (experienced) eye, and your own instincts.

## 3.13 Additional Tools for the Online Portfolio

### Portable document format (PDF)

The PDF file is a commonly used hyperlink for web-based portfolios, supplementing HTML (Hypertext Markup Language). The Adobe Acrobat® program creates PDF files that capture and preserve all the fonts, formatting, graphics and colour of any source document, regardless of the application and computer platform used to create it. To view or print any PDF files you can download for free the software application Acrobat® Reader from the web. The beauty of a PDF is that any document can be converted to a PDF file from within any application by simply sending a print command, with PDFWriter selected as your 'printer'.

### Audio

Speech (or dialogue), music and sound effects are three broad categories of audio component. Just like every other design element, audio layers have to support – not distract from – the prime message. Just because you can add sound doesn't mean you should.

Sound editing and design software should be used wisely and for a specific reason. Once you have completed your sound recordings, you can drag and drop individual files into your web pages. Beware that since the recording must be stored as a file, it is usual for a short clip to be repeated in an endless loop, which can create an irritating experience.

### Video clips

Video clips of your design work especially 3D modelling can add a lot to your online portfolio if they are well produced. The advantage of video is that you can layer audio clips, video clips, still images and text. If possible, use a digital camcorder because the footage is already computer-ready. Because digital video is, like cinematic film, made up of many still images large files are required. Usually this is about 30 frames per second (fps) for videos. However, on the internet you may get acceptable results at 10–15 fps, though action and zooming might look a little jumpy. To show your video clips on the internet they must be compressed and saved as Quick Time MOV or MPEG files. Software tools are required if you want to edit or mix your shots, add soundtracks and special effects, make titles, and so on. The most important rule is to keep video clips short because they will be a more favourable viewing experience compared to longer ones.

### Animation

Animation and simulated 3D environments allow viewers to see your work in ways not possible with a traditional portfolio. Multimedia tools allow for the creation of 360° panoramas from photographs or computer models, and enable the examination of objects in the round. Depending on the focal length of the lens used to shoot them, 12–18 images are needed to generate a panorama.

## 3.14 Case Studies

Portfolios created by Sam Chermayeff, Cathlyn Newell, Openshop, PellOverton, and Hilary Sample show a variety of intentions, levels of formality, styles, contexts, and aims. However, they all present information in an organized and accessible way. Some of these portfolios are structured along strictly linear sets, or linear with branches or sub-themes. There may be many subordinate parts to the overall design, but all of these are related to a dominant theme.

Sam Chermayeff tries to control the pace of the viewer. By constantly shifting the view from macro to micro level he achieves a unique visual rhythm. The switch in scale creates drama and emphasises the mobility of his design.

Cathlyn Newell's portfolio layout addresses the interrelated issues of proportion and scale. Every relationship is developed in the same way: from general to specific, from large issues to small issues, from essential form to elaboration in details.

Openshop utilize the widest range of available mediums – even the 'obsolete', which in itself is a statement of inclusivity (and fun) – to reach the widest possible audience. Their workbooks are designed for clarity, there is no jargon. The uniform dimensions of the workbooks supports the individualized cover imagery that becomes part of a close-up of texture, enlarged and cropped.

The portfolio of PellOverton is characterized by playfulness, but also a rigorous structure and investigation. Among formats for distribution are booklets. These mini-portfolios have become works of design in their own right. They embody the company's achievements and current preoccupations.

Hilary Sample tackles large issues first. Abstracted geometry is used to form large blocks on the page layout. This method is an alternative to the grid. By establishing a geometric relationship the large issues are resolved first, leaving the smaller issues of scaling, cropping, typeface etc. to be addressed later on.

# Sam Chermayeff

**1.**

**How would you describe your portfolio-making process?**

I would liken my portfolio-making process to making a musical composition. I think carefully about where to place crescendos and where to let harmony play on.

**2.**

**Do you use your portfolio as an inventory or archive of your work?**

The portfolio is an inventory. The best part is that the act of making the portfolio asks me as a designer to think about what to do next, and I appreciate that opportunity.

**3.**

**Do you organize by agreement or meaningful oppositions?**

I organize based on graphics rather than content. This can be anything such as:
Small thing – Small thing – Big thing – Small thing
**or**
Colourful – Colourful – B&W – B&W
**or**
Focused – Broad – Broad

While on the one hand we need to find threads to follow, we also need to engage the person who is flipping through our portfolios, particularly when that person is not reading or even understanding but is just having a peek. For this reason I make high and low points in my portfolio, and think carefully about where I should make someone view on a macro level and where to offer a micro level. There is an uneven pace and it is the balance of these points, and the in between, that give order to what might appear a random portfolio.

**4.**
## Is your portfolio primarily image-based or is it primarily text-based?

My portfolio is entirely image-based even if there is some text-based explanation. I don't expect anyone to read the words. That said, the text can be a graphic part of the portfolio, even if no one reads it.

On a side note, this may be the difference between books and portfolios. Books require reading. Portfolios have to be able to be understood in some way without reading.

**5.**
## Is your portfolio primarily design-driven or is it project-driven?

My portfolio is design-driven (though it is nothing but a collection of projects). The order and feel are determined by a desire to create an attractive rhythm from the available images and words of my projects. The design 'problem' is about tone and changes therein, that is how to keep people visually engaged.

**6.**
## How do you gauge the effectiveness of your portfolio?

I have made many portfolios over the years, all for a specific purpose. I have both failed to get the job and won the job. This may be the only way to determine the effectiveness. Certainly the best portfolio begot the best job. Another way to judge effectiveness would be just how much and for how long I enjoy my portfolios. My last one, made nearly five years ago, was a deeply loved and oddly fetishized item at the time of its creation. About a year later I found it embarrassing, but since then I've come to consider it a lovely snapshot of an earlier time.

**case study**

MAY, 05'

THIS IS MY MOST RECENT PORTFOLIO, LEFT TO
RIGHT STARTING WITH THE COVER. NO TEMPLATE.

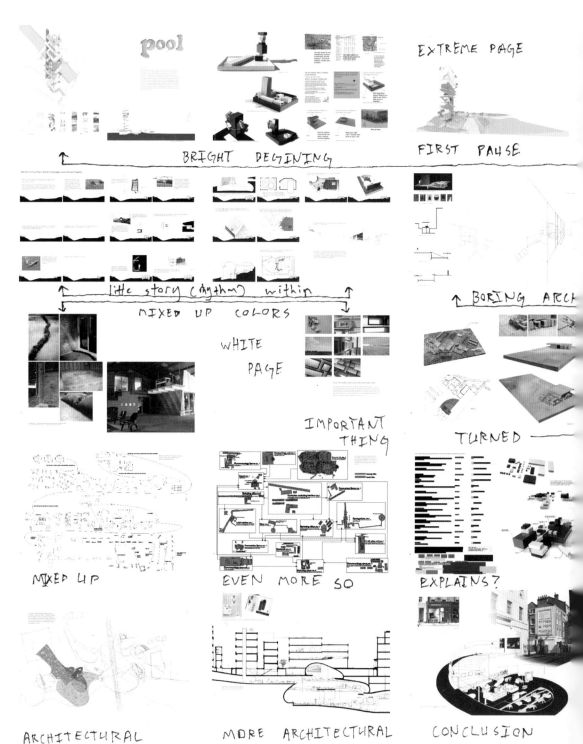

EXTREME PAGE

FIRST PAUSE

BRIGHT BEGINNING

little story (rhythm) within
MIXED UP COLORS

BORING ARCH

WHITE PAGE

IMPORTANT THING

TURNED

MIXED UP

EVEN MORE SO

EXPLAINS?

ARCHITECTURAL

MORE ARCHITECTURAL

CONCLUSION

I'VE TRIED TO IMAGINE THIS SPREAD
AS A VISUAL SCORE. I'VE LOOKED
AT FORM RATHER THAN CONTENT.

small

BIG

WHITE
PAGE

ENT (MIDDLE)↑ ↖ ↙A LULL
IS OK.

IMPORTANT
THING

>STRAIGHT ————— >TURNED / STRAIGHT

(A KIND OF PAUSE)

EXTREME PAGE

HNICAL
ESUME + MISCELLANY

FUN

FUN----->ARCHITECTURE

little thing
that I
could give
up

IF I MADE A NEW
PORTFOLIO I WOULD
ADD THIS AT THE
END FOR A LOUD
FINISH.

A SETTING TO HOLD THE READER.

PAUSES ARE IMPORTANT IN A PORTFOLIO. MINE, AS SEEN ON THE PREVIOUS SPREAD IS FAIRLY EXUBERANT THROUGHOUT BUT HAS SEVERAL BREAKS. THE GENERAL STATE IS MUCH LIKE THIS SPREAD.

S A STARTING POINT THIS IS AN EXAMPLE OF INTUITION
AKING PRECEDENCE OVER RATIONALITY. FROM HERE A RHYTHM
AY EMERGE.

THE TWO PAGES BELOW ARE THE BREAKS. THEY
MAKE THE READER STOP, IF ONLY FOR AN INSTANT.
FOR ME THESE ARE THE TWO MOST IMPORTANT
SPREADS. THEIR CONTRAST FROM THE REST DEFINES
THE RHYTHM.

FINGER FOR SCALE

# Cathlyn Newell

## Strategy

The portfolio was submitted as the major point of reference for the inaugural SOM Foundation prize and travel fellowship for architecture, design, and urban design. Considering the generous sum of the award, and the intention to travel and research for approximately 1 year, the overall strategy was to present the work as a body of related, yet varying, investigations on a larger overall theme – a theme that was to continue during the proposed fellowship work. Each project was therefore selected as an articulation of both personal interests and methods, as well as a demonstration of overall tendencies and past studies.

The Foundation required (or preferred) that the submission be presented in a 3-ring binder. The intention was to allow for pages to be removed or pinned up, but perhaps it was also a means to deter strange packaging or over-the-top cover systems often submitted during such a competition, and to allow instead the work to speak fully for itself.

## Production

Overly picky about line-weights, colour, and texture of prints, I decided to print the pages myself giving the capacity for instant reprints and adjustment as needed. Tweaks and compositions were made through Adobe Illustrator and InDesign based on the structure of existing files and the quarks that always emerge with large, graphically complex files. The work was produced with an Epson inkjet printer on semi-gloss photopaper. Not an easy corner store find, the 11" x 17" binder was tracked down online and has a non-descript matt-black finish. I stuck a print-out of my identity number on the exterior to complete the overall package, and I used the numbering system as a simple marker and identity graphic.

**Advice**

- If you don't like your portfolio, no one else will. Allow the style of your graphics and your personality to show through.
- Establish a format and aesthetic that carries throughout the entire book. Rules can be broken because projects need to find their own methods, but a solid backbone of graphical tricks will bring projects together as a cohesive set.
- Know your audience. The layout must be such that someone who does not know your work can quickly and easily understand where different projects or sections start and end, and how they tie together.
- Become obsessive with print quality, colour appearance, and legibility. It can be time consuming but overwhelmingly significant and rewarding.

case study

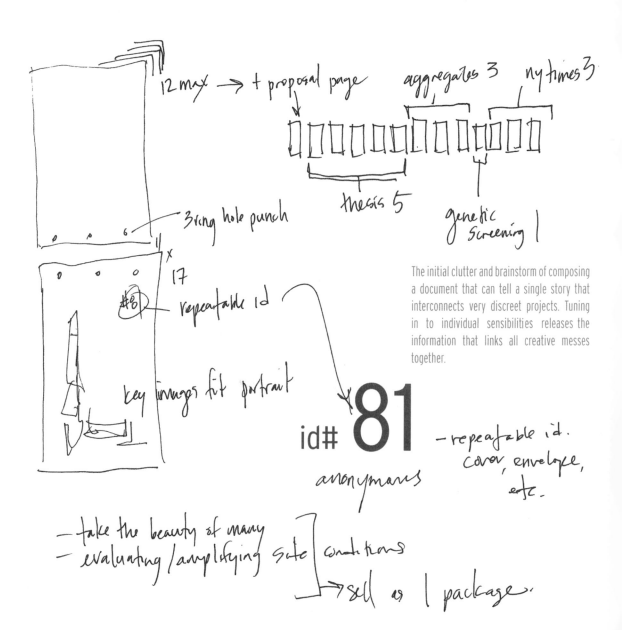

12 max → + proposal page          aggregates 3    ny times 3

3ring hole punch

thesis 5                    genetic
                            screening 1

The initial clutter and brainstorm of composing a document that can tell a single story that interconnects very discreet projects. Tuning in to individual sensibilities releases the information that links all creative messes together.

17

repeatable id

key images fit portrait

id# **81**

anonymous

— repeatable id.
cover, envelope,
etc.

— take the beauty of many
— evaluating / amplifying site conditions
        → sell as 1 package.

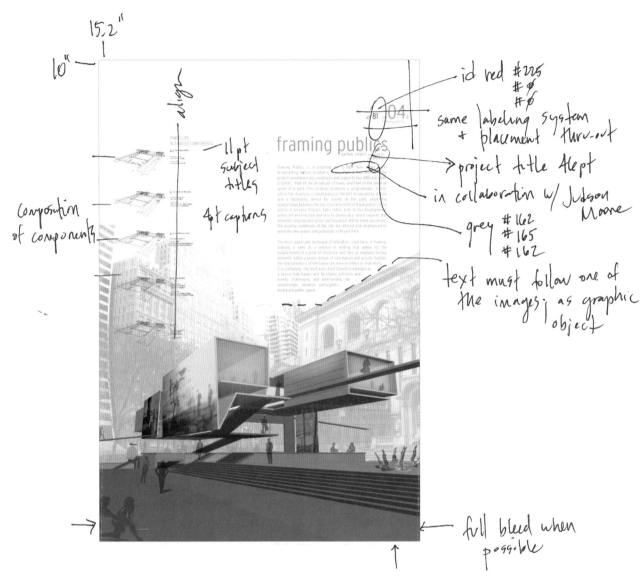

The composition of each page must tell a focused and direct story of the project at hand. However, graphical links and patterns stitch an entire set of works together.

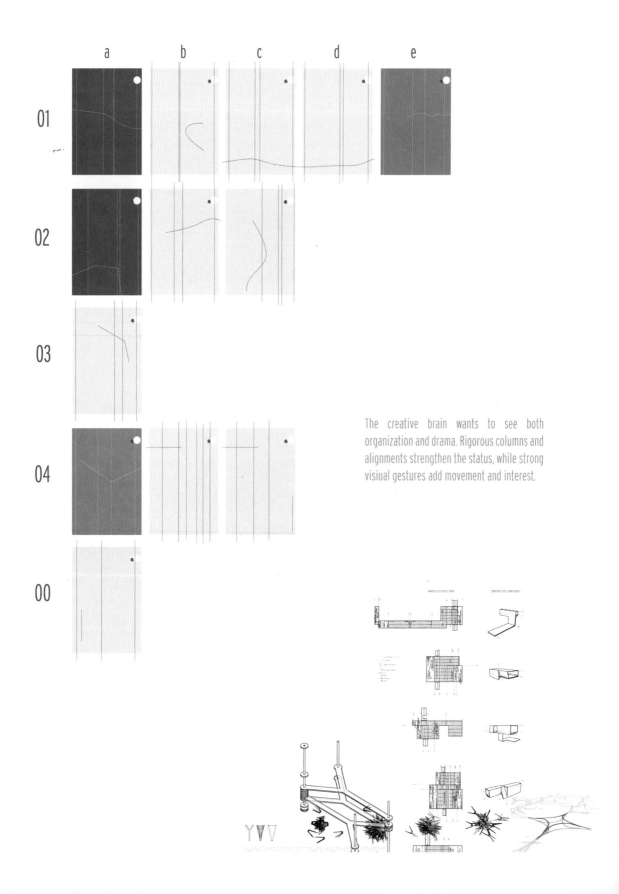

The creative brain wants to see both organization and drama. Rigorous columns and alignments strengthen the status, while strong visisual gestures add movement and interest.

a    b    c    d    e

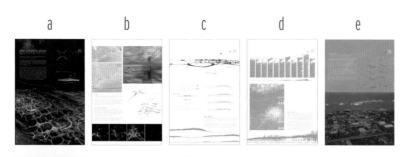

thesis 01
site amplification

fabrication 02
aggregate

scripting 03
genetic screening

building design 04
framing publics

proposal 00
site registration

With previous work serving as the primary basis to apply for a large research and travel based fellowship, key to the portfolio was the desire to present a body of work that demonstrated a larger idea already explored in various methods and scales with room still for growth. Simultaneously, and just as important, the portfolio need to support the intention for travel and research that displayed efforts to contribute to the field of architecture through these means.

The SOM Foundation provided constraints from which to launch decisions as well. At the time, the requirements included an established format of 11x17 pages. Reviewing the already composed images, collages, and documentation it became apparent that a portrait layout was necessary for key images already present in the work. An additional set requirement was that of 3-ring binder; reducing the stress of contemplating a cover and binding system but emphasizing the importance of each page telling it's own story. This constraint, along with a 12 page maximum standard established the need for project information and sequencing to be on every page, eliminating a page in essence wasted on a table of contents. The weight of each project was evaluated in terms of depth of research and discussion, further developing sequencing strategically for graphics and importance as opposed to a chronological presentation.

The portfolio has since served as a backbone for more presentations. Pages have been added.

new pages +
additions + updates

+

+

+

# Openshop

## Strategy

Our portfolio consists of workbooks which each distills a project down to the process from start to finish. In many ways the workbooks serve as working documents for the process of Openshop. They are meant to communicate to us internally as well as, externally, to clients, peers, and really anyone who is interested in how we work. As such, we have been known to continually change and evolve our portfolio so that it reaches many mediums and many audiences. In fact, we have just completed a portfolio that is shown on an old TV run by out-of-date iPods and iPhones.

## Production

We use every type of media available to us, and each project is simultaneously considered in 3D, sketches, spreadsheets, models, mock-ups, etc.

**Advice**

Tips for portfolio making are always tricky because it is a personal communication about whom and what you are. So our advice is to always make sure it clearly communicates what you are. 'Clearly' is the operative word. Also, a portfolio need not be the typical architect's portfolio – architects seem to be good at communicating only with other architects.

**case study**

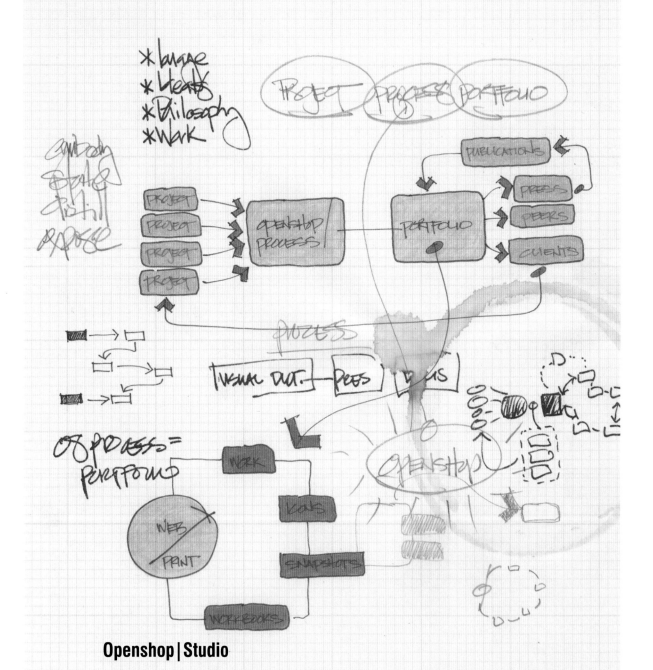

## Openshop | Studio

At its core Openshop is driven by a process that lets a problem become a point of view and a point of view a solution. It is the way two partners assimilate their own views and the needs of clients into new ideas. Every project is filtered through this methodology to create a unique solution. As a result the body of work and the process itself are in a constant state of evolution and flux. The idea of Openshop's portfolio, is conceived similarly, as an ecology of elements that can grow and evolve to represent a constantly advancing world view. Its elements, online and in print, aggregate in different ways, creating multiple feedback loops to tell the story of Openshop.

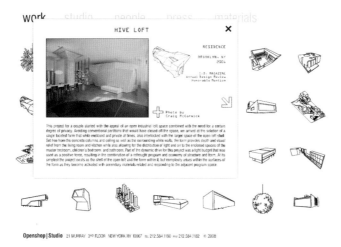

**WEB/ICONS/SNAPSHOTS**

**PRINT/WORKBOOKS**

# Anatomy of a WORKBOOK:

The WORKBOOK is the base unit of the portfolio ecology. It is a retrospective look at the facts and processes of a project following its completion. Its purpose is both documentary and representational, as it serves as the platform for presenting a total body of work to prospective clients, the press and to peers. Its components disperse beyond the workbook itself to populate the web site or to be re-distributed for specialized marketing.

While every workbook evolves to best represent a particular project, there are specific underlying elements that form the structural underpinnings of every workbook. This allows the collected workbooks to represent the scope and voice of Openshop.

## Cover

An axonometric logo is paired with a name for each project. It is used on workbooks and in the web site to access and identify the individual works. Each workbook is also covered with a detailed image of a material that best personifies the project.

## Data

Basic project data is presented in conjunction with an iconic image and a general statement that positions the project.

## Process

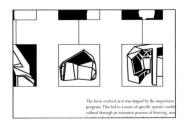

A selection of the conceptual work that led to the project conception is represented to re-present the design process. This is accompanied by an anecdotal text flow in red at the bottom of the page that offers insight into the source of many of the design decisions.

## Selected pages from Hive Loft:

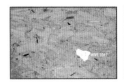  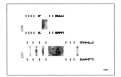  

**Cover**          **Data**                              **Process**

### Documentation

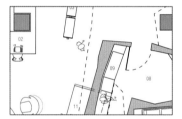

Plans, sections, elevations, etc. show the project in basic architectural terms. This is the elemental representation that serves as a platform for understanding the intentions behind any project.

### Construction

Photographic documentation of the construction process captures the concept becoming the object.

### Photographs

Final photography is the definitive opportunity to see the whole and the parts working together. It is both a documentation of what was done and a chance to frame and summarize the work.

**Documentation**         **Construction**         **Photographs**

# PellOverton

## Strategy

We keep two types of portfolio in the office. The first is an archive of our work that we use for presentations to clients. This portfolio is designed to demonstrate the breadth of our experience (project types, size, and working conditions) and is organized for maximum impact on a non-professional audience. To that end, the work is not typically polemicized in this format.

The other portfolio is more of an ongoing project: a shifting body of work and research that represents the theoretical ambitions of the office and the material directions that this ambition takes. This work is summed up at various moments by stand-alone booklets which aim to position a selection of projects around a specific set of themes. Sometimes these booklets are produced for awards submissions or competition entries, but they are also, more regularly, snapshots of our current preoccupations. In that sense, the 'project of the portfolio' is a continuous effort, which is manifested through a variety of mini-publications that work as status reports along the way. We generally produce these booklets in bulk and distribute them to colleagues and others with whom we feel our practice is in dialogue.

The voice of the portfolio is articulated through the introductory statement and the project descriptions. These are intended to establish a critical framework through which the shared interests of the various projects can be understood. This framework generally takes the form of a loose historical and theoretical context and, like the work itself, is intended to express a rigorous methodology – but not without some humour or irony.

## Production

We use a digital single lens reflex camera and imaging software to make our portfolios.

## Advice

Experience has shown us that a portfolio is not simply a scaled-down version of a larger presentation or a print version of a website. The portfolio is a book, which is different from a website or a wall of large-format images, and requires that we think in terms of how books are assembled, stacked on a shelf, and – hopefully in the case of our portfolio – occasionally opened and read. This affects everything from the size of images and type, to the best structural hierarchy for the presentation of each project, and to the overarching narrative of the book. The fact that one must choose between delivering content as a spread or a single sheet changes the way one might present a project.

**case study**

**pelloverton**, New York  (Ben Pell and Tate Overton)

*At a time when many young practices are operating under the banner of 'multi-disciplinary' practice, we are interested in reaching outwards to find new ways to return to center.*

*This statement should not be confused with a retreat to architecture's disciplinary autonomy. On the contrary. Rather than branching-out or crossing-over, we attempt to identify sensibilities which architecture inherently and/or approximately shares with outside models. Terminology, techniques, and tools that might belong conventionally to graphic design (composition and content), industrial design (digital fabrication, mass and custom production), or textiles design (wallpaper, pattern, shape and fit) are adopted and assimilated into our practice, and instrumentalized to closely examine issues that are very much at the center of our own discipline.*

*The projects included here have each developed from an emerging methodology of reconnaissance - a loose genealogy of historical moments and cultural artifacts newly curated into a contextual tableau for our work. In all cases, the curatorial stitch is understood as one or more shared sensibilities; a lens through which we can reconsider architecture's fundamental assumptions. For example: converging template-based dressmaking with digital fabrication to pose a new relationship between home and body, or engaging the nature of architectural 'finish' as both spatial and programmable.*

*This approach has enabled our work to resonate with models both contemporary and historical, and with sartorial, landscaping, and visual traditions, among others. Rather than being 'multi-disciplinary', our practice benefits from a disciplinary resonance embedded within our process; one which establishes a conduit for ideas between parallel yet distinct disciplines of form and performance.*

The portfolio is an ongoing project in our office, representing the theoretical ambitions of our practice and the various material directions that these take. These efforts are summed up at various moments as stand-alone booklets which aim to position a selection of projects around a specific set of themes. Often produced for awards submissions or competition entries, the booklets provide regular snapshots of our current preoccupations. The voice of the portfolio is articulated through the introductory statement (left) and the project descriptions. These are intended to establish a critical framework through which the shared interests of the various projects can be understood. This framework generally takes the form of a loose historical and theoretical context, and like the work itself, is designed to express both a rigorous methodology and a typically amused approach to the projects and our practice.

cover

project image

walldrobe / wearpaper

Each project begins with a full-page, full-bleed image: either a detail of the design, or a found image that represents an aspect of the project.

**garment to garment**

10mm NICKEL FINISH WIRE SNAPS
part #124904 (use setter #810200)

**garment to wall**

#2 x 1/4" STAINLESS STEEL
FLATHEAD WOOD SCREW

The images in the portfolio serve multiple roles: at times documenting the projects (plans, sections, and elevations); in many cases illustrating the presumptive experience of the projects (model photographs, renderings); and as analytical devices which describe the conceptual and material organizations of the project (diagrams - such as the above images)

This installation was designed in response to an invitation to exhibit our work at a for-profit gallery on the Lower East Side. Rather than mounting models on pedestals and presentation drawings on the wall, we proposed an installation which could demonstrate our ongoing curiosity and exploration of atmosphere, surface, and fabrication. Looking to situate these pursuits within the context of a gallery which has traditionally shown paintings, we turned to the 19th century paintings of Caspar David Friedrich and Gustave Courbet, as well as 20th-century color field painting for models of similar sensibilities towards figure and field, surface and atmosphere. The result is an installation which attempts to generate visual and material affinities between the surfaces of the gallery, the work on view, and the occupants, essentially operating in two different modes, Passive and Aggressive.

**graphic behavior**

The Aggressive mode of the exhibit brings the figural qualities of the installation to the foreground through the deployment of four wall types - assembled, printed, planted, and reflective - which were allowed to overlap either visually or physically throughout the gallery to establish a sense of movement and a network of affinities. For example: peace lilies growing through the planted wall were reproduced as graphic patterns that would glow through the printed wall; the reflective finish stainless steel bar and folded planes of the dropped mylar ceiling would conflate the red glow of the printed wall with the textured surface of the assembled wall, as well as projecting the images of passersby on the street through the storefront and into the middle of the exhibition.

In its Passive mode, the installation serves as background for other activities and exhibits in the space by providing both mood and discrete shape to the long, narrow gallery. The installation re-conceives the gallery as two spaces, small and large, which can function separately or as a continuous and singular room, aiding the curation of different types of work or multiple shows running simultaneously in the gallery. The Passive mode of the exhibit also enables us to address in part the for-profit nature of the gallery: by providing a creative enclosure for activities like release parties, book launches, and other design-related celebrations, the installation becomes a catalyst for revenue; essentially acting as an elegant cocktail dress for the gallery - a conversation piece that is less about itself and more about generating mood in the room.

Opposite the full-size introductory project image is the project description. This text begins with an explanation of the cultural, historical and/or theoretical background for our approach to the project, and is accompanied by three or four reference images or diagrams with which we feel the project can be identified. These images are not always refered to directly in the project brief, but help to visually describe a broader discursive field from which we are borrowing techniques, forms, or sensibilities in the given project.

opposite: detail of model, view of installation through storefront

1. *Color Field Painting*, Philip Taaffe, (1983).

2. *A Thicket of Deer at the Stream of Plaisir-Fontaine*, Gustave Courbet, (1866).

3. *The Wreck of the Hope*, Caspar David Friedrich, (1824).

passive aggressive

GRAPHIC B[

**pelloverton**
architecture research group

fiberglass panels    vinyl wrapped    back-lit

elevation of overall installation

image by day: a blurred view of Stamford from the eyes of a commuter

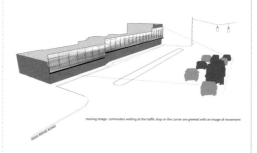

HIGH RIDGE ROAD

moving image: commuters waiting at the traffic stop on the corner are greeted with an image of movement

surface by night: fluorescent strips illuminate panels from behind to mimic movement of headlights below

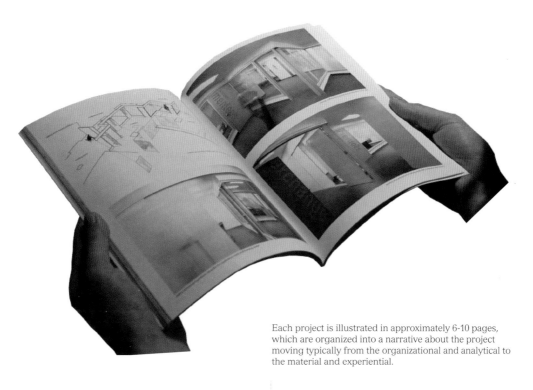

Each project is illustrated in approximately 6-10 pages, which are organized into a narrative about the project moving typically from the organizational and analytical to the material and experiential.

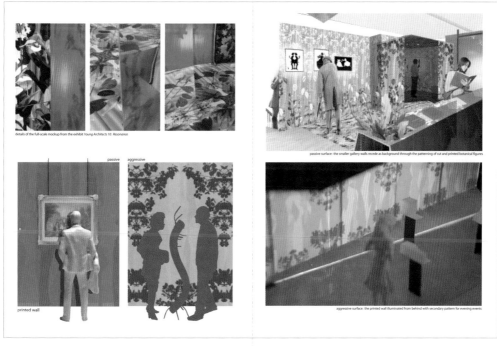

details of the full-scale mockup from the exhibit *Young Architects 10: Resonance*

passive surface: the smaller gallery walls recede as background through the patterning of cut and printed botanical figures

passive    aggressive

printed wall

aggressive surface: the printed wall illuminated from behind with secondary pattern for evening events

## Hilary Sample

### Strategy

Along with producing models, renderings, drawings, films, and mock-ups in the office, we create a graphic manual or book to accompany each project. These studies form an integral part of the design process. I produce these books at different stages of the project: they are mainly for our use as a critical means of looking at our work. The portfolios always have a clear organization: a beginning, a middle, and an end. There are always several layers, and a series of introductory images. This organization requires a careful questioning of the goals of the project, and a written text that describes the project is always found in the beginning. This written text is always the most difficult part of the portfolio, and requires the most time. We will rewrite the introductory statement several times before finalizing it. The title is also something that we work on for a very long time. It is tested graphically on the cover to see if it works. The process is not linear. The process is repetitive, and each book is produced over and over again, including printing, binding, and editing. Each page is thought about in relation to the overall structure of the book, and in relation to the other pages. Often the book's structure is found through the repetition of mocking up the book. Each iteration becomes more refined and rigorous. No book ever looks the same, and no structure is ever repeated. The process is repeated but the end result is always different. Every portfolio is unique. I am against a standard format.

### Production

The production of the book or portfolio is always the same. There are 6 steps:

1   **layout** the project in Adobe InDesign
2   **insert images** – often new images are needed and content must be developed and this is developed through model photographs, Illustrator diagrams, line drawings, film stills, and digital renderings
3   **insert the text**
4   **print at full scale**
5   **edit**
6   **repeat**

**Advice**
Print at full scale and in colour.

# Afterparty, PS1/MoMA, Young Architect's Program, 2009

This project is entitled Afterparty, a proposal for the Young Architect's Project competition. The design booklet, which was presented at the time of the interview presentation, also includes models, material samples and construction drawings. The booklet is formatted for 11" x 17" pages and follows a specific set of guidelines for placing margins, headings, texts and sub-texts in proportion to one another. The book is divided into three parts: cover with design introduction, design, and construction details and budget. Each section is separated by a bold graphic text on a black background. The book is 60 pages.

**Sketch Model**

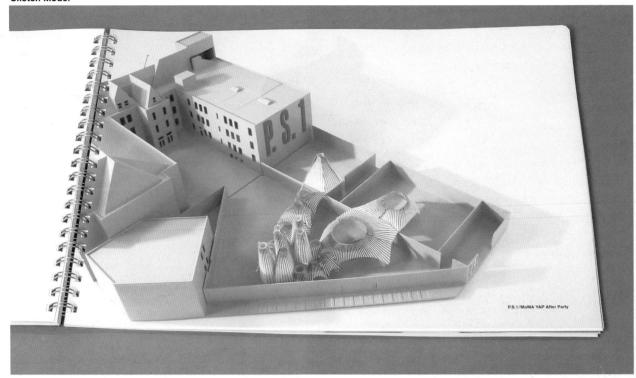

**Book Cover**

**Perspective Drawing**

**Model Photo**

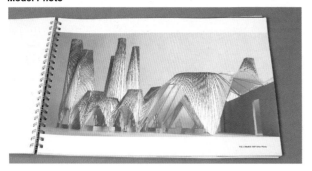

**Program Diagram**

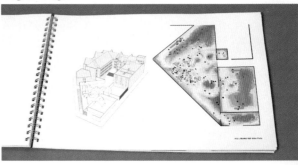

# ART ARCHIPELAGO, Ballroom Marfa, 2008

The Art Archipelago project is a unique project in the office as it combines both architecture and landscape. The challenge of the portfolio was to find ways to illustrate the large scale of the 8 acre site, and at the same time present images of the drive-in theater screen. The selected images show the screen structure set in the park, and are further illustrated with sketches, renderings and precedent images. The final image is a construction mock up and drawings made specifically for the mock up.

## Design Statement

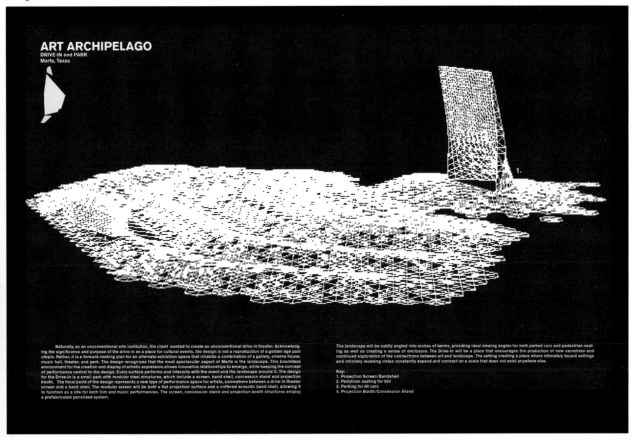

### Perspective Rendering

### Mock-up Photograph

# Ambient Architecture, Thesis Project, Princeton University, 2003

This booklet is a working design ideas presentation for a student thesis project. The book presents all aspects of the project, from research including plant studies and environmental analysis to physical and digital drawings and renderings of the proposed architecture. The organization of the book is as follows: introduction of the site [drawings and maps], climate and atmosphere analyses, program analysis and ideas, studies for the form of the building and details of a thermally active facade system. The booklet specifically works through scales from large to small, from urban to facade detail.

**Perspective Rendering**

**Book Cover**

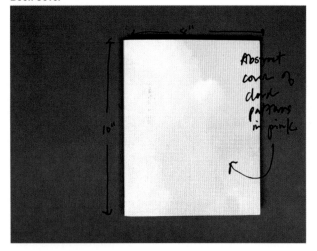

**Design Statement**

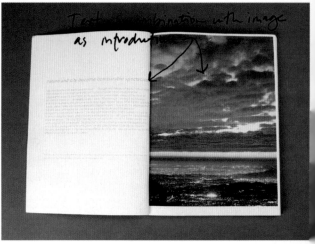

# Portfolio Structure, Thesis Project, 2003

This portfolio was made as a design research tool. Its structure consists of a repetition of large blocks that are subdivided according to content. Large blocks introduce and close the project whereas subdivided pages present a combination of images and renderings along with descriptive texts.

**Front Cover**

**Introduction**

**Full Panorama**

**Details**

**Details**

**Back Cover**

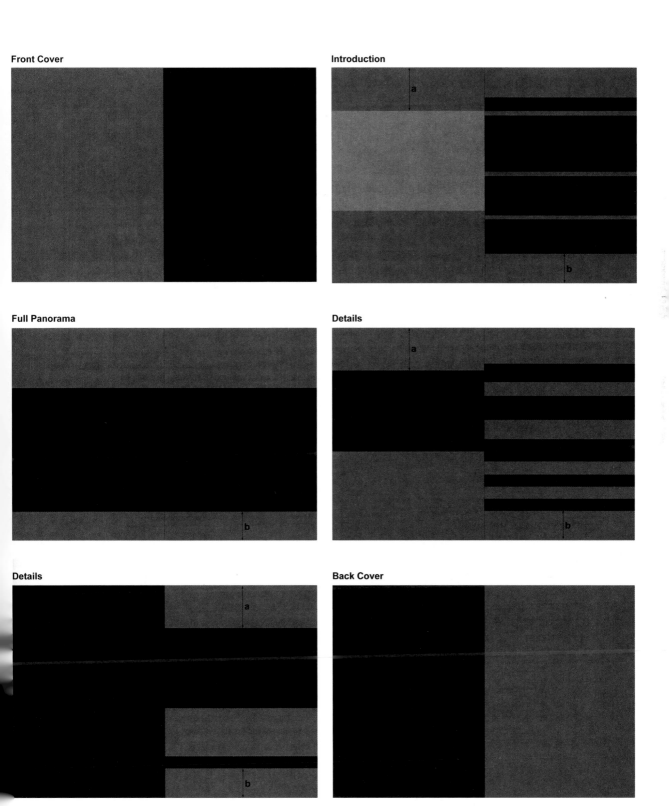

# 4

# Send It, Present It, Market It

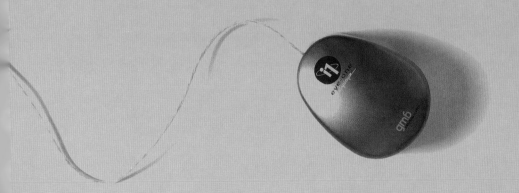

## Send It, Present It, Market It

What is marketing? Marketing is connection, exchange, and dialogue. It involves the circulation of information (in the form of ideas and things) and the establishment of value. The portfolio is a marketing tool for gaining access to opportunities and experience in both the academic and professional worlds. The specific contents of the portfolio change to reflect the momentary intention of the presenter based on the perceived needs of the receiver. Marketing is also an act of translation: translation of our interests, skills, and character into the language of an audience.

## 4.1 Networking

The job now becomes presence, profile – whatever you want to call it. We can maximize exposure, presence, and reception in many ways. Be on as many radar screens as possible. Try to find people inside – and even outside – the business or industry you are interested in to serve as your advocates. This is a time to tap into as many contacts as possible. There are good opportunities that anyone can take advantage of.

**Meet people at:**
- studio open houses
- trade shows
- self-initiated events and exhibitions
- local, national, and international competitions
- job fairs
- lectures
- conferences

**Cultivate the following:**
- media contacts
- peers, mentors, and former teachers
- established clients

**Consider the following activities:**
- Exchange links with friends, distributors, blogs, etc.
- Initiate/participate in exhibitions and events covered by local newspapers and media (they often post links in their online articles).
- Submit your website to search engines and website directories.
- Join industry-related forums.
- Attend public lectures and receptions.
- Subscribe to professional list serves, discussion groups, and newsgroups.
- Submit articles and press releases to websites that are looking for content, making sure the articles have contact information and website links in them.
- Develop search-engine-friendly keywords, phrases, and meta tags.
- Build links to other websites, web directory categories, niche websites, online press releases, and reviews.
- Join social networks, write blogs, and twitter.
- Attend professional conferences.

**Conduct research in the following:**
- subject areas outside of architecture
- alumni magazines
- professional journals

- local institutions
- web searches (general, specific)
- links
- list servers
- admissions catalogues

The golden rule of networking is that you never leave a meeting without at least one referral.

**Talk**

Being able to talk about your work is one of the most important things you can do as a successful architect. We create ideas that can be seen visually, but we have to be able to explain them clearly to others. Prepare talking points (a maximum of 5) about your work, your ideas, and your ambitions so that you are always ready to engage someone with brevity and clarity.

## 4.2 Informational Interviewing

Don't be afraid to call or write to a design studio, agency, or corporation which attracts you. It is particularly important to look for a position that really interests you. Making the right kind of inquiries (finding out to whom you should be talking and whether it's appropriate to contact him/her directly) may lead to an informational interview during which you can learn about the firm's character and exactly what it is looking for in an applicant. The primary goal of the informational interview is an inside look, but you will want the conversation to help you reach secondary goals as well. These are:

- finding out about potential jobs
- making potential allies/advocates
- practising your interview and presentation skills

**Unsolicited queries and submissions**

People are busy. Respect their time. Find out what they do so you know if your work is suitable for them before sending anything. Think about what you want to ask before you call, and write it out, just bullet points. Practise your lines a few times until you are sure of what you want to say. Be concise, tactful, direct, and understanding. Follow up with a mailer!

**Leave-with copies and 'Thank you for your time' notes**

You should have at least one good-quality photocopied or printed brochure or mini-portfolio of your work to leave with clients as a reminder of your style and your contact information. You can store this in the back pocket of your portfolio, or send it to the client with a 'Thank you for your time' note after your portfolio call is completed.

**Mail shots**

Send printed samples of your work (a single postcard, a short leaflet) regularly to friends, colleagues, companies, or others whose interest you want to cultivate. This is an inexpensive and effective form of advertising because of its simplicity and good natured persistence.

## 4.3 Sending Your Portfolio

If your designed layout is to be posted out, it must fit into an envelope, so the design may be affected by the way in which it will be posted. Be sure it conforms to postal standards, the same goes for your SARE (self-addressed return envelope).

Remember, everything means something. For example, yellow string-and-button envelopes are used for internal post and carries with them the implicit message of work-related papers / bulk items / and other 'undesirables'. Be sure that the packaging is secure and keeps your portfolio in pristine condition. Bristol board or light-gauge cardboard sheets are good for keeping paper contents from creasing in transit.

The final step is not complete until your portfolio reaches its destination without mishap or damages. Before you post anything do the following:

- Make sure it is addressed correctly, and it is directed to the appropriate person.
- Check that the postage, tracking system and insurance are sufficient.
- If the recipient is expected to return the portfolio it's essential that the self-addressed return envelope includes sufficient (local) postage or international postal reply coupons.
- Be sure your return address is on your envelope in the upper left hand corner. Mail handlers will always appreciate type written labels. Handwriting will do, but it should be a very readable style.
- Many submissions will not be returned. Make sure you know what the return policy is before you send anything that you hope to get back.
- Always pre-test your labels. Many pens (particularly felt pens) have water-soluble ink which will run if exposed to humidity or rain.
- Copier and printer ink runs when it's wet. Cover envelope labels with a strip of clear packing tape, neatly trimmed and smoothly applied.

**Several portfolios ready to go**

It's useful to have several portfolios that are set up for different purposes: for example, a universal portfolio, a narrowly focused skill-set portfolio, and general-purpose portfolios tailored for individual clients. Supplement these portfolios with pages that the client will find useful for their particular needs in addition to online portfolio web pages.

## 4.4 The Interview

### Interview: a two-way dialogue

Interviews may be conducted by the principal alone, or with staff; or by a panel consisting of administrative staff, and sometimes other students. Each office and institution is different. The amount of time an interview will take is usually 30 minutes. The interview is a two-way process: they want to see what your skills and interests are, and you usually have the opportunity to ask questions and to have a look at working spaces and facilities.

### The X factor

You only need to understand how quickly you can assess someone's personality and character traits, to realise how quickly and instinctively potential clients, employers, and admissions officers (as people) respond to you. It's genetic, a requirement of survival for cave people and architects. Ultimately it is the most important and the least controllable of all variables.

### Feedback

Ask for criticism at the end of the selection or interview process (if you are not offered the job). It requires a detached fearlessness – although if motivated by a genuine interest in feedback this contact can be enormously beneficial in pointing out the shortfall between intention and actual effect. Furthermore, the interviewer may be surprised to find a very different person sitting before him/her because of the new context. Reviewing your feedback about your portfolio will help you improve the quality of your future design work. It is the final step in the interview process and the first step for a new portfolio.

## 4.5 Gauging the Success of a Portfolio

'Congratulations. You have been selected.' 'The job is yours.' These are the words we want to read and hear. We look at our portfolio with intense satisfaction and perhaps awe. Clearly it has done its job. It's a success. Conversely, 'We regret to inform you… .' The portfolio has failed.

Gauging the success of a portfolio depends on how we define and use it (and there are many ways depending on our needs at a particular time). As self-reflective lifelong practitioners dedicated to the very unpredictable nature of architectural practice we have reason to integrate audience response with our own account towards an overall assessment of our portfolio.

The learning process inherent within the portfolio is that of work created in a series. Each portfolio solves certain problems, and suggests issues to be dealt with in the next one. Viewed this way the success of the portfolio can be gauged by how it gives us the ability to experiment, to value and learn from mistakes, and build on experiences.

Consider terms of success:

- What has been learned?
- What actions might follow?
- What are the implications for future portfolios?
- How will the knowledge gained be used?
- How will it be integrated?

**Be passionate and be persistent**
Even if you don't get the job, stay in touch with the company's or department's managers. That way, you may be at the top of the list the next time there is an opening. At least you'll have established a relationship. Besides, the first 30 days of a new job are always difficult. The new appointee may not stay, and you could be right there in the wings. Finally, be prepared for some rejection by having a back-up plan. Use the rejection to create positive plans that will help you achieve your dreams.

## 4.6 Case Studies

In this chapter case studies of DnA_Beijing, CEBRA, Alan Dempsey of NEX, Gage / Clemenceau, and Kawamura-Ganjavian offer hard evidence of problem solving by graphically revealing the depth of the firms' experience. The portfolios go beyond mere discussion of a topic. They are catalysts for self-presentation and self-promotion in a highly competitive global market. DnA_Beijing's presentation philosophy emphasizes the observation, the unassuming, the simple and direct. The tactile quality of every component is crucial to their dialogue with clients.

CEBRA's simple and direct approach is designed to create an easy experience for readers. Their book is almost purely visual, with movement conducted by extreme contrasts in density from page to page. It excludes 'ornamental' graphics which they consider a distraction from the illustrations.

Gage / Clemenceau's luxurious, custom-tailored portfolio is an openly seductive, multi-sensual experience. Concerned with the 'unique and real' highly individualized design approach, they use mostly high-quality photographs of work, with little text.

Alan Dempsey of NEX uses a variety of media to gather a diverse audience: books, articles, exhibitions, lectures, and temporary installations. Meticulous project layouts transmit the tone and character of the office. The portfolios (print and web) are conceptualized as generative channels, not stopping points.

Kawamura-Ganjavian's web portal serves double-duty as up-to-date self-publicity and as a stable archive organized to highlight completed works. 'Digital dossiers' are pdf versions of mail-shots profiling individual projects.

**DnA_Beijing**

## Strategy

Be unique. Present it well. Look at graphic designers. Build up a list of graphic designers who you like and can draw inspiration from. They design booklets and layouts for a living, but we as architects can take big clues from what they do and how they do it. Colour schemes and layouts can be adapted, but always keep it simple. And keep it personal. This could be the one opportunity to present to potential clients. Don't force ideas on people. Stand out and be unique. But don't start off by striving to be unique; it will come with development of an initial idea.

We try and carry out a theme for each particular portfolio that we do, maybe focusing on particular elements such as detailed design. Look at new and unique layouts, but factor in the cost and ease of production too. Most importantly, just absorb the inspiration around you.

## Production

You want to stand out, don't confine yourself to glossy images. Use cheap photocopies, but present it well and think about the information you are displaying. Sometimes you will want to come across in different ways. For low-cost housing schemes, perhaps use low-cost materials, but crafted in an expert way to represent where your talents lie. If you do use photocopies, bind them in a simple coloured card with a basic title on the front. People are more likely to pick up yours and read it than the thousands of glossy publications which lie on the table in front of them. The tactile quality of everything here is crucial; shiny in my experience often can come across as cheap. Don't be overly ambitious. Often the portfolios which stick in the clients' minds, are the well-made simple ones, which do not look like the others.

**Advice**

- Don't act like you think you know it all, absorb the criticism of others. There is always something new to learn.
- Don't force it, let it come naturally. If you are aiming to get it done within a set time period, give yourself enough time.
- Look around you – newspapers, magazines, posters etc. – for inspiration like layouts and small details.
- Get it wrong and learn from your mistakes. No one gets it 100 per cent correct.
- Make a scrapbook of interesting layouts and styles you see in newspapers, magazines, etc. so that you can take influence from them when needed.

case study

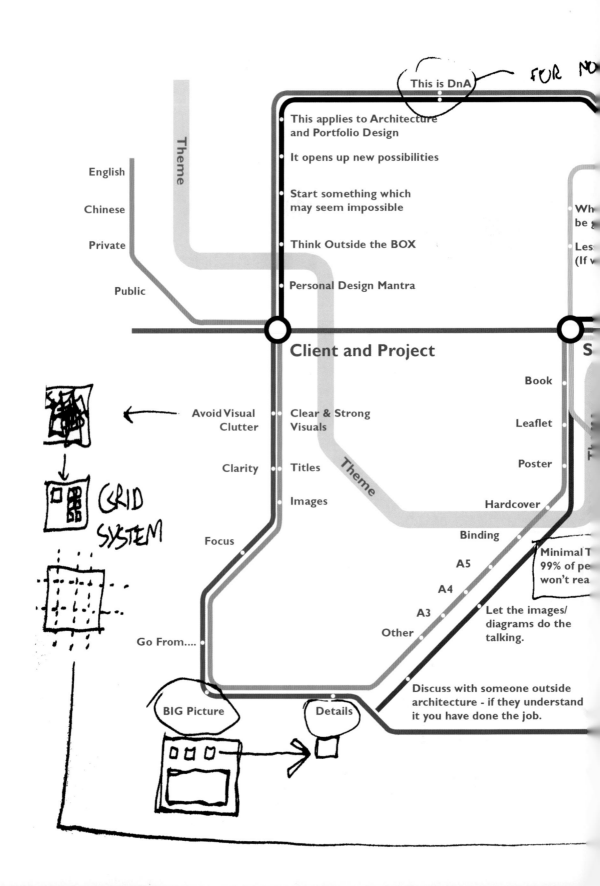

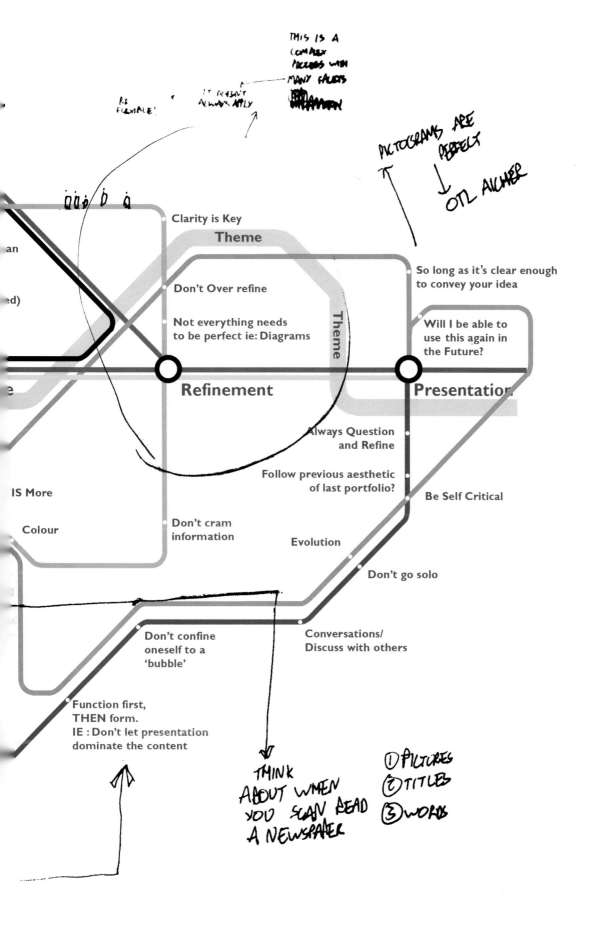

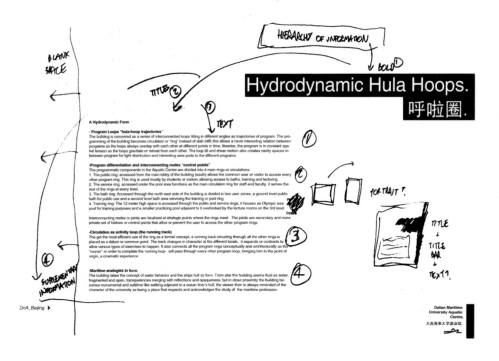
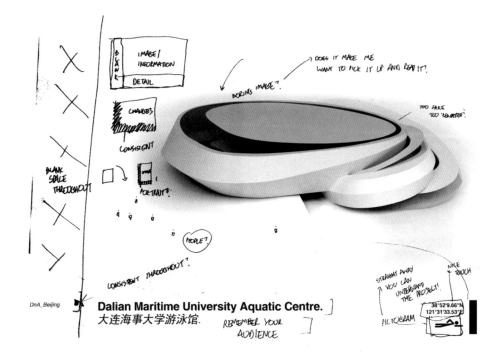

Dalian Maritime University Aquatic Centre.
大连海事大学游泳馆.

Hydrodynamic Hula Hoops.
呼啦圈.

Dalian Sports Centre.
大连市民健身中心.

Sports Station.
运动中心.

# CEBRA

**1.**
**What are your inspirations and influences?**
For the book *CEBRA_files_01* the main inspiration is Le Corbusier's oeuvre.
It is a very systematic way of showing architectural work – almost like looking into a filing cabinet. This makes it easy to make numbers 2, 3, and so on. You simply slide another project into the layout matrix.

**2.**
**Do you keep many portfolios? What distinguishes one from another?**
Up until now we have just done the first *CEBRA_files_01* but another is on the way in 2010. For special customers there is a version 1.5 going around with projects completed after the number 1 and too prestigious not to show. When we retire I hope there will be at least 5 volumes.

**3.**
**Is your portfolio designed as a summation of your current preoccupations or is it designed as a continuum of your work as a whole?**
Our book describes the oeuvre of the office until 2006. But when we apply for competitions and show more recent works we create special mini-portfolios which are focused towards the specific job.

**4.**
**Do you use your portfolio as an inventory or archive of your work?**
Yes – very much, and this is exactly why we named it *CEBRA_files_01*.

**5.**
**Is your portfolio a stream-of-consciousness?**
Well, in our portfolio we simply went through all our work starting with the first project and then crossing out the projects that were either unfinished, too small, or whatever. Then we created the book with the ones left standing, chronologically arranged. It is very simple, methodical, and, most of all, fast and therefore cheap!

**6.**

**Is your portfolio primarilydesign-
driven or is it project-driven? Is
it primarily image-based or is it
primarily text-based?**

It is almost all images. We are not big
writers so we rely on the architecture itself
to communicate to the public. There is a
good long interview in the book though.

**7.**

**How do you gauge the
effectiveness of your portfolio?**

You know, to be perfectly honest, we did
the book mostly for our own sake, but it has
been lying around in book shops around
the world since Actar found it interesting
enough to distribute. This makes me believe
that it has had some effect in making a
name for CEBRA.

**case study**

Front and back

Content

## CEBRA_FILES_01

In 2006 we decided to publish a 400 page book with our projects dating back to when we set up the office in 2001. We were self assured enough to call it CEBRA_files_01 since we expected it to be the first in a series of books to come. We still do, and the work on the second one is soon to be undertaken.

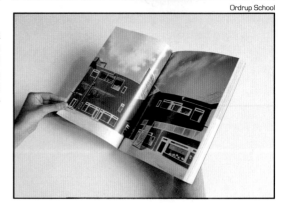
Ordrup School

Water School

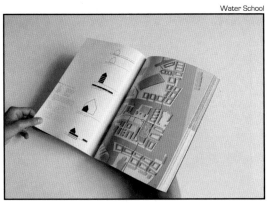

Loop House

Water School

Music Theatre

Kongehallen

The book is divided into two sections. The first one – much shorter than the second – is graphically dry and monochrome. It contains text only and describes the philosophy behind our work primarily through an interview. It also accounts for factual office data such as CVs and staff information. The book is bilingual with Danish texts printed black on white for left pages and English written as white on black for the facing ones. In contrast to this rather straightforward section the rest of the book – some 95 percent of the pages – are vivid and highly colorful. This is where the actual architecture is displayed via all kinds of diagrams, sketches, renderings and photographs. The images are kept within a layout frame that consists of three standard compositions and only the absolutely necessary information, such as square feet and completion dates are given. But even so flipping through this section is like turning a kaleidoscope.

Kongehallen

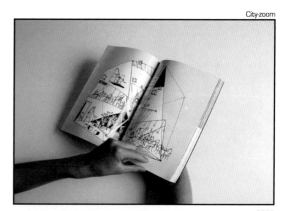

It is an abundant collection of illustrations that would feed greedy eyes for quite some time.

CEBRA_files_01 is very much like a traditional portfolio in the sense that all the projects are ordered chronologically as sheets in a simple folder. It doesn´t have an extra layer of ornamental graphics or anything else that could draw away the attention from the architecture itself. We create an experience and sort of guide the readers into the spaces we´ve designed - it´s as simple as a family album and hopefully as present - it´s a reminder of Rossi´s famous saying that "architecture is architecture".
Website: www.cebra.info

Harboørehallen

Villa Strata

A stack

Front Data

# Alan Dempsey, NEX

## Strategy

Our ambition for a discursive mode of operation extends beyond our architectural projects and we try to unfold this architectural discourse through other media, such as books, articles, exhibitions, lectures, and temporary installations. Indeed if the history of architecture is any guide, architectural enquiry is often at its most complete when articulated through media other than itself. In this context, we do not view the portfolio as a simple representation of our work but instead treat it, and graphic media in general, as another channel to advance our design thinking and document acquired knowledge as a growing body of research.

## Production

Two ongoing graphic projects that communicate the work of the office are our printed office profile and our online presence. The office profile is a small loose bound document that is flexible enough to be updated on a monthly basis. It has a simple structure and layout and is designed to communicate our office ethos and selected work to the widest possible audience, including potential clients, consultants and staff, and is also used for more formal tender submissions.
Our online presence was used as an opportunity to explore a more complex curatorial approach to our work. One of the frustrations we find with a printed portfolio is the limited ability to make dynamic connections across the work – to show the ways in which specific ideas develop from one project to the next and are revealed in different ways from one media or application to another, i.e. research, competitions, books, exhibitions, conferences, and of course through representations of a building itself. Once a printed document is organized in a particular way it is difficult to reorganize.

Our website explores the potential of digital media to dynamically associate one piece of information to another, and in doing so becomes slightly more representative of the way we work. It is organized into 5 sections of news, office, work, media, and contact, and each has their own sub-sections. However, individual content items are also cross-linked in a more dynamic way using semantic relationships. The site was designed and built in collaboration with media agency Despark.

**Advice**
Developments in digital fabrication and design to production processes have placed renewed emphasis on the building as object and the physical presence of architecture. At the same time, the production and consumption of architecture as a cultural and artistic practice have proliferated across an ever wider range of media. Each of these brings their own specific forms of representation, the use of which we believe can bring new insight to specifically architectural problems.

case study

Our office focuses on the intersections between architecture, infrastructure and urban design. Our name, NEX, refers to our approach of placing ourselves at the centre or nexus of a design and delivery process that links clients, collaborators and fabricators through integrated computational and technical platforms. Our integrated design process explores new generative potentials in architecture while also increasing efficiencies during project delivery, and our rigour allows us to work across multiple scales and sectors in international contexts. We aim to produce work that is a coherent expression of the social, cultural, economic and environmental conditions specific to each project while contributing to a wider architectural discourse.

Our ambition for a discursive mode of operation extends beyond our architectural projects however and we try to unfold this architectural discourse through other media, such as books, articles, exhibitions, lectures and temporary installations. Indeed if the history of architecture is any guide, architectural enquiry is often at its most complete when articulated through media other than itself. In this context, we do not view the portfolio as a simple representation of our work but instead treat it, and graphic media in general, as another channel to advance our design thinking and document acquired knowledge as a growing body of research.

Two ongoing graphic projects that communicate the work of the office are our printed office profile and our online presence. The office profile is a small loose bound document that is flexible enough to be updated on a monthly basis. It has a simple structure and layout and is designed to communicate our office ethos and selected examples of work to the widest possible audience, including potential clients, and in more formal tender submissions.

Our printed portfolio or profile presents our vision, design approach and selected projects. Each section is laid out over a double page spread. The left hand page contains the section titles and a descriptive text in two columns. The right hand page an image or images that reflects and reinforces the text content.

APPROACH

APPROACH

01 Our design approach is illustrated with images from two recent projects which show how we manage information models from early concept through to production.

02 A selection of images of our team and consultant partners shows our collaborative approach to our work.

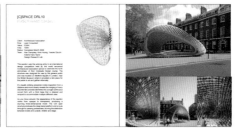

RESEARCH

[C]SPACE DRL10

03 Research is a central process in the office, and a selection of images from the FAB programme at the Architectural Association give some insight into this.

04 A short text describes the concept and materialisation of each project. Drawings, visualisations and images of the completed work complete the description.

**DODDER BRIDGE**
Infrastructure, Dublin

Client: Mountbrook Group & Dublin City Council
Role: Lead Consultant
Value: £1.5 Million
Span: 32m
Status: In progress
Team: Alan Dempsey, Filippo Previtali
Adams Kara Taylor

This pedestrian and cycle bridge was won through an international open design competition and is being commissioned by the Mountbrook Development Group as part of their regeneration of a major site in Ballsbridge, Central Dublin. The bridge is being constructed as part of a comprehensive community gain package and when in place, it will complete the revitalisation of the local pedestrian and cycle network.

The concept of the bridge is to create a hybrid of infrastructure and public amenity by providing generous seating and deck width across the span for pedestrians to pause and enjoy the views of the river.

The structural design accommodates the constraints imposed by river channel clearance so the main central spine passes above the deck on the lower south bank creating the extended seating area. The structure is fabricated off site from rolled steel plate and aluminium and painted a vibrant light blue.

The projects section of the book is laid out in a similar manner. The title, project type and location are on the left hand page above key project data, and a short descriptive text. A diagram or drawing that describes the central concept of the project is placed adjacent to this text. The right hand page is given over to images of the project.

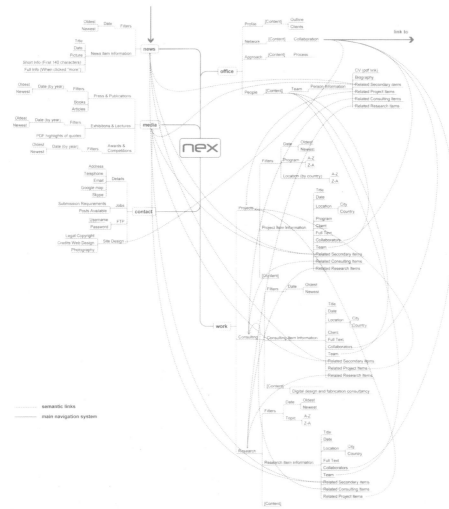

**www.nex-architectrure.com**

Our online presence explores a more complex curatorial approach to our work. With a printed portfolio there is a limited ability to make dynamic connections across the work: to show how specific ideas develop from one project to the next. These ideas could be conceptual, material, or structural and technical approaches, but once a printed document is organised according to any one, then it is not easily reorganised.

Our website explores the potential of digital media to dynamically associate one piece of information to another, and in doing so becomes slightly more representative of the way we work. It is organised into five sections of news, office, work, media and contact and each has their own sub sections. However, individual content items are also cross-linked in a more dynamic way using semantic relationships. The site was done in collaboration with media agency Despark.

main navigation bar
background image
content filter bar

content panel

content item

item preview image

The homepage of the website is formatted like a news blog. All the latest posts in different sections of the site are assembled here as short items. Clicking on any item expands it for more information and links to the relevent section of the site.

01 Our design philosophy and approach are outlined in the office section of the site. A random image of one of our projects is displayed in the background.

02 A short profile of each team member is followed by a list of the work they have been involved with. A list of other related items from the news blog follows.

03 Projects are summarised in small panels. A thumbnail image captures an important concept of each project and the name, type, location and date are also listed, so projects can be easily reorganised by any category.

04 Selecting a project brings up a more detailed description and a selection of images describing the work. The content panel can now be hidden to allow full appreciation of the images.

# Gage / Clemenceau Architects

## Strategy

In an age of ubiquitous information and imagery, cheap home printing, flash websites, and self-published vanity monographs, the portfolios from Gage / Clemenceau Architects aim to be actual and unique objects. In opposition to this ubiquity of imagery, our portfolio formats are never repeated, are uniquely luxurious to the touch, are rarely discarded, and above all are intended not only to inform the recipients of the content of the work produced from the office, but also to transmit some of the sensational, tactile, and aesthetic ambitions for which the office is known.

## Production

Every portfolio produced in the office, whether for a potential client, award submission, publication, grant application, or other endeavour, is custom tailored towards that particular audience or person. Images are selected from projects and combined to illustrate a particular valence of the work, geared towards the recipient. Each page is printed as an individual plate on archival quality 350gsm watercolour paper, and is contained, along with the other plates, in a 13" x 19" laser-cut archival photography box. Depending on length, the printing cost of a single portfolio can exceed $1,000, requiring us to be exclusive in who we prepare them for. The expense and effort that this requires forces us to consider our opportunities in a very careful way – leading us to produce portfolios for only the projects, applications, and awards that we are truly interested in pursuing.

**Advice**

I encourage my students, when laying out
their portfolios, to reference the El Croquis
books. They are great at mixing drawings
and images into an incredibly descriptive
look at a project or architect. They also
seem to remove a lot of the fluff that
populates architects' own monographs.
I'm on the admissions committee at Yale
and one thing that has stuck with me is that
portfolios today are much less about work
than personality. I actually think this is a
bad development. We make our portfolios
about the work – images of the work mostly.
I also dramatically limit the amount of
diagrams included, as I believe that a lot of
architects today rely on the graphic quality
of their diagrams to justify their work instead
of having the work do all the work, so to
speak.

case study

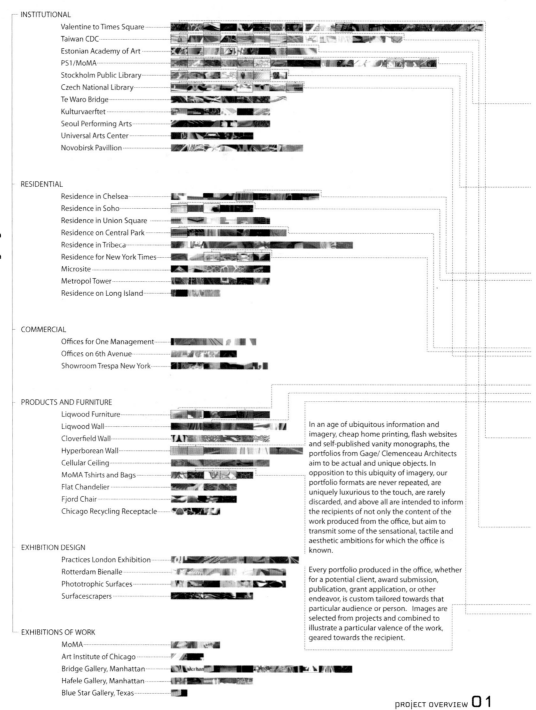

GAGE / CLEMENCEAU ARCHITECTS

INSTITUTIONAL

Valentine to Times Square
Taiwan CDC
Estonian Academy of Art
PS1/MoMA
Stockholm Public Library
Czech National Library
Te Waro Bridge
Kulturvaerftet
Seoul Performing Arts
Universal Arts Center
Novobirsk Pavillion

RESIDENTIAL

Residence in Chelsea
Residence in Soho
Residence in Union Square
Residence on Central Park
Residence in Tribeca
Residence for New York Times
Microsite
Metropol Tower
Residence on Long Island

COMMERCIAL

Offices for One Management
Offices on 6th Avenue
Showroom Trespa New York

PRODUCTS AND FURNITURE

Liqwood Furniture
Liqwood Wall
Cloverfield Wall
Hyperborean Wall
Cellular Ceiling
MoMA Tshirts and Bags
Flat Chandelier
Fjord Chair
Chicago Recycling Receptacle

EXHIBITION DESIGN

Practices London Exhibition
Rotterdam Bienalle
Phototrophic Surfaces
Surfacescrapers

EXHIBITIONS OF WORK

MoMA
Art Institute of Chicago
Bridge Gallery, Manhattan
Hafele Gallery, Manhattan
Blue Star Gallery, Texas

In an age of ubiquitous information and imagery, cheap home printing, flash websites and self-published vanity monographs, the portfolios from Gage/ Clemenceau Architects aim to be actual and unique objects. In opposition to this ubiquity of imagery, our portfolio formats are never repeated, are uniquely luxurious to the touch, are rarely discarded, and above all are intended to inform the recipients of not only the content of the work produced from the office, but aim to transmit some of the sensational, tactile and aesthetic ambitions for which the office is known.

Every portfolio produced in the office, whether for a potential client, award submission, publication, grant application, or other endeavor, is custom tailored towards that particular audience or person. Images are selected from projects and combined to illustrate a particular valence of the work, geared towards the recipient.

Images are selected and organized specifically to illuminate particular areas of the practice for a focused audience. While the images are custom selected and combined, a general layout template forms a cohesive structure in which any collection of images and text can be combined into a realizable whole.

Each page is printed as an individual plate on archival quality 350gsm watercolor paper, and is contained, along with the other plates, in a 13" x 19" laser-cut archival photography box. Depending on length, the printing cost of a single portfolio can exceed $1,000, requiring us to be exclusive in who we prepare them for. The expense and effort that this requires forces us to consider our opportunities in a very careful way-- leading us to produce portfolios for only the projects, applications, and awards that we are truly interested in pursuing.

Each portfolio is custom laser- etched with the recipents name on the cover. The printed plates, in order to avoid excess shifting during transport, are collected and bound by a ribbon that can be cut or untied by the recipient.

The completed portfolio, pictured to the right, was produced as Gage / Clemenceau Architects was nominated as one of thirteen international firms, for the inagural Ordos Prize in Architecture. The full document contains 37 custom plates that illustrate both speculative and built work, as well as writings, press and other descriptive aspects of the firm.

# Kawamura-Ganjavian

## Strategy

We use the web portal as a communication tool for a wide audience. It is kept updated on a very regular basis in order to inform of our professional whereabouts as well as of our latest projects, endeavours, media clippings, and achievements.

The web portal works also as an archive of our work, displayed under a selected highlighted group and under a complete works group that depict images, drawings, and project profiles of our different initiatives (territorial, spatial, products, academic, and research).

Our dossiers are readily available formats that are categorized in different editions (products, exhibition design, and architecture) that correspond to our main lines of work. These files (pdfs) contain a selection of our work and are updated on a quarterly basis and they are optimized for web use (download and emailable).

Both our web page and our dossiers follow a clean aesthetic with an easy-to-read lay out that summarizes the main ideas of each project without getting trapped into irrelevant details.

## Production

The self-managed web portal and digital dossier are produced with commercially available graphic software packages.

**Advice**
The web portal is our way of communicating our whereabouts and our latest news to a wide audience. It is important to keep it updated on a regular basis. Our dossiers, classified by type of work and updated on a quarterly basis, do not have numbered pages so that they can be custom-edited for specific clients, providers, institutions, etc.

case study

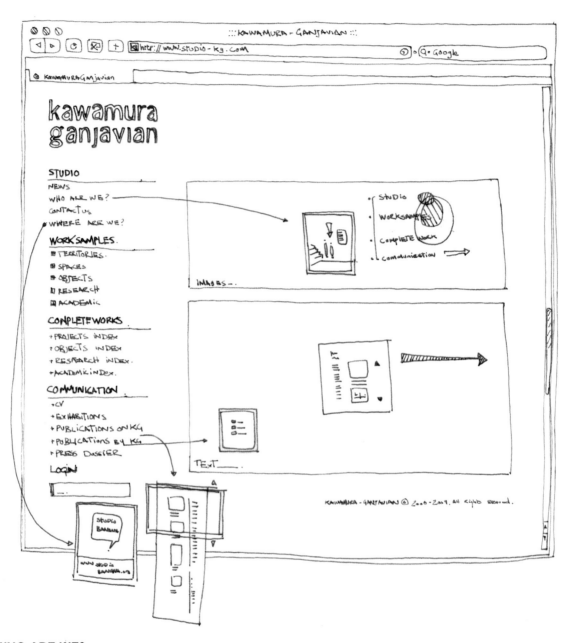

## WHO ARE WE?

kawamura-ganjavian is a young architecture studio established in 2000 by Key Portilla-Kawamura and Ali Ganjavian. After meeting in London, where both were studying, they have worked in several countries India, USA, Japan, Great Britain and Switzerland in the fields of urbanism, architecture, stage design and product design, both professionally and academically.

In 2006 they set up their present base in Madrid from where they direct projects in Spain, Great Britain, France and Switzerland.

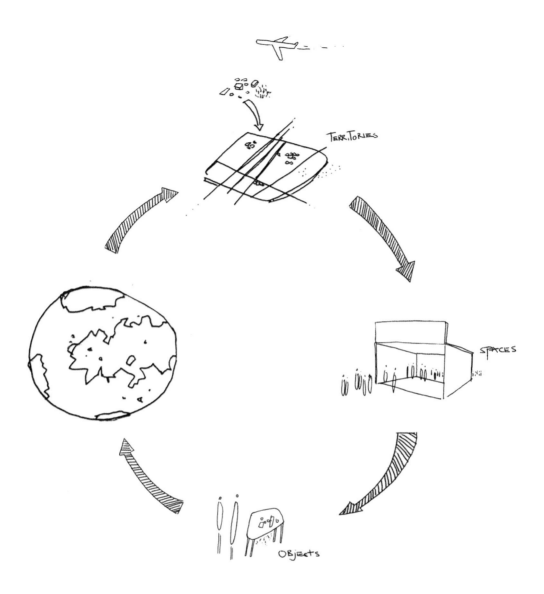

They are founding members of the multidisciplinary creative platform Studio Banana.

In spite of its youth, and in virtue of the intense experience of its members in some of the most prestigious academic centres (Royal College of Art London, Cooper Union New York, Architectural Association London, Istituto Europeo di Design Madrid, Accademia di Architettura di Mendrisio) and architecture studios (SANAA Tokyo, Herzog & de Meuron Basel) of the world, the studio has the capacity to take on board architectural challenges at all types of scales.

kawamura-ganjavian are also Milos Jovanovic, Sofie Liesenborghs, Mónica Mejía and Agustín Zea.

**STUDIO BANANA**

**PLATFORM FOR INTERDISCIPLINARY CREATIVITY**

*Project Titel.*

Renovation project, 2007

Madrid (Spain)

Built surface
394m2

Budget
135.000 EUR

Client
Studio Banana S.L.

*REF DATA.*

Studio Banana is a multidisciplinary platform dedicated to creativity in its broadest sense. Kawamura-ganjavian were not only the designers of the space but also the founders of the platform. The project consisted in the transformation of a dilapidated print room in the basement of a 1960's residential building.
The result is a luminous and generous space with multiple and flexible uses that is used both as a workplace by numerous young creative professionals and as a catalyst of cultural activity in this part of Madrid.

*Project concept + Aims objectives.*

## PSYCHIATRIC CLINIC

Schematic design 2008

Aravaca, Madrid (Spain)

Built surface
4.630m2

Budget
9.500.000 EUR

Client
Clínica López-Ibor S.L.

A psychiatric clinic is primarily a house for feeble people on their way back towards a normal life in everyday society. It is like a mini city with different sections, ambients, streets...
The client of this project, the third generation of a renowned psychiatric doctors family, had in mind a complex programme with multiple users (serious patients, casual patients, patients' relatives, medical staff, service staff, residents) which was accommodated using a clean and simple array of architectural means. Given the nature of the building (psychiatric consultation rooms and day hospital) and the natural slope of the site, the building is arranged in terraced wings with different medical functions that profit from the individual gardens they each have. The treatment of the planting and open spaces is exquisite, becoming an inherent part of the therapeutic process.

# Postscript

# Postscript

What will be the essence of a portfolio in the future? What will be its properties, boundaries, and traditions? The portfolio will develop as tools from the letterpress to the computer have developed, creating models as varied as a sequence of pages (linear) and hypermedia (non-linear, 3D). The future of the portfolio can be considered exciting with the extension of the use of applied typography and image generation and manipulation.

As a collection of visual information the portfolio as presentation format is perfectly matched to a global culture increasingly measured out in images. It is a locus for the transmission of ideals, values, and, if nothing else, norms. It is also a methodology with which we can set our work in the context of our own intellectual and imaginative development. Part recording and part dialogue, the portfolio is both a summary of one's experience and a marketing tool. In other words the portflio offers hard evidence of problem-solving and answers the 'show me' demands of employers.

When we make our thoughts concrete in a portfolio we open ourselves to judgement. We gain confidence, clarity, and an assessment of our work. By identifying the implications of each step in the portfolio-making process and exploring the possibilities for the mechanics and ideals of portfolio-making in this book it is hoped that readers will find new sources of intellectual and creative stimulation.

In closing, I would like to say, again, that the portfolio is a beginning, not an end in itself. It is a methodology for self-evaluation and development, and an ongoing invitation to grow.

# Types of Portfolio

**Type:** Admission
**Description:** Also known as an application portfolio, required to enter many higher education programmes. There is a distinction between an application for an undergraduate course and a postgraduate course. However, in both cases you are asked to present 12–15 pages of your best and most recent work. In most cases an admissions committee is in charge of reviewing portfolios.
**Audience:** Higher education

**Type**: Artist
**Description**: Also known as a 'book', a selection of work, used to display an artist's skills and achievements to a specific audience. The style of the portfolio is determined by the medium which the artist uses. For example, slide portfolios are still the preferred way to show paintings and drawings for review. However original work is usually required to demonstrate printmaking and photographic capabilities.
**Audience:** Prospective clients, established clients

**Type:** Autobiographical
**Description:** 'Tell me something about yourself'.
**Audience**: Self, prospective clients, established clients

**Type:** Award
**Description:** Also known as a fellowship portfolio, documents the various approaches, successes, ongoing refinements, and excellence of the design work. In most cases this portfolio form is restricted to a page limit.
**Audience:** Professional organizations

**Type:** Competition
**Description:** Used as an entry for a competition or as a submission of a design proposal for an actual development. Some competitions are open, others are restricted by invitation only. Architectural competitions have become popular in Europe as a means of selecting architects for public projects.
**Audience:** Public, government, not-for-profit organizations

**Type:** E-portfolio
**Description:** An electronic version of a portfolio designed to demonstrate skills which may include inputted text, electronic files, images, multimedia, blog entries, and hyperlinks using dynamic formats. The e-portfolio is popular in higher education because it can facilitate students' reflection on their own learning, and lead to greater awareness of learning strategies and needs.
**Audience:** Higher education

**Type:** Exit
**Description:** Measures the quality and dimension of work on an undergraduate course.
**Audience:** Higher education

**Type:** Experimental
**Description**: A visionary portfolio defining its own standards.
**Audience:** Self, prospective clients, established clients

**Type:** Expertise
**Description**: An organized collection of complex, performance-based evidence that indicates current knowledge and skills in a particular role or area of expertise.
**Audience:** Prospective clients, established clients

**Type:** Grant
**Description:** An application for monetary funding to execute a particular project.
**Audience:** Government, not-for-profit organizations

**Type:** Interview
**Description:** A polished selection of documents representing a candidate's best work and accomplishments, used in the job-seeking process.

**Audience:** Professional companies, government and not-for-profit organizations

**Type:** Matrix
**Description:** An unabridged collection of past work as well as work in progress using a template.
**Audience:** Professional organizations

**Type:** Mini-portfolio/mailer
**Description:** A mass-produced abbreviated version of a more complex and comprehensive portfolio. An abbreviated introduction to your work, it can be used as an initial contact with professional companies or graduate schools. It should be easy and affordable to reproduce.
**Audience:** Professional companies, government and not-for-profit organizations

**Type:** Original
**Description:** Used for job interviews, gallery submissions, marketing presentations. It is not sent through the post or left with others.
**Audience:** Professional companies, government, not-for profit organizations

**Type:** Personal
**Description:** An album, notebook, scrapbook, or collection of documents and artefacts demonstrating a particular interest, journey, passion, field of study, etc. in any medium (film, photo, video, etc.).
**Audience:** Self, friends, relatives

**Type:** Professional
**Description:** Communicates primary characteristics and auxiliary dimensions (specific skills) of work, i.e. your value to a prospective employer.
**Audience:** Professional companies, government, not-for-profit organizations

**Type:** Project
**Description:** Documentation of a project or area of independent study.
**Audience:** Education

**Type:** Scholarship
**Description:** A candidate's portfolio for tenure and promotion based on 3 categories: teaching, research, and service.
**Audience:** Higher education

**Type:** Student
**Description:** A demonstration of accomplishments for a class/tutor group.
**Audience:** Education

**Type:** Teaching
**Description:** A selection of artefacts and reflective entries representing a teacher's professional experiences, competencies, and growth over a period of time. It can be used as an extended curriculum vitae.
**Audience:** Education

# Schedule

The average schedule (in days) presented here is based on best practice, but is by no means the only approach.

| 1st step | 1st step | 3rd step | 4th step |
|---|---|---|---|
| **Contextualize It** | **Plan It, Select It** | **Design It, Produce It** | **Send It, Present It, Market It** |

| | | | |
|---|---|---|---|
| | Understanding yourself | Mock-ups Dummies | Distribution |
| | Identifying your audience | Design Layout Structure Styles | Promotion |
| | Conserving work | Squint test | Collect feedback |
| | Selecting work | Production | |

0   1   2   3   4   5   6   8   9   10   11   12   13   14   15   16   17   18

# About the Portfolio Contributors

### Dimitris Argyros
Born in Athens, graduated with first-class honours degree from the Bartlett School of Architecture, University College London. Employment: Arup Associates, Professor Sir Peter Cook, Professor C. J. Lim, Wilkinson Eyre Architects.

### CEBRA
A Danish architecture practice based in Århus, founded by Mikkel Frost, Carsten Primdahl, and Kolja Nielsen (2001). CEBRA has realized a wide range of building projects and has won a number of architecture competitions, including the Golden Lion at the International Architecture Biennale in Venice (2006) and the Nykredit Architecture Prize (2008).

### Sam Chermayeff
Born in New York, graduated from the Architectural Association (2004) and the University of Texas at Austin (2005). Joined SANAA (2005).

### Alan Dempsey, NEX
NEX is an architectural design office founded by Alan Dempsey in London with an international profile. The practice focuses on the intersections between architecture, infrastructure, and urban design, and our name, NEX, refers to our approach of placing ourselves at the centre or nexus of a collaborative design process that links clients, consultants, and fabricators through integrated computational and technical platforms.

### DnA_Beijing
DnA_Design and Architecture is an interdisciplinary practice addressing our contemporary living environment, both physical and social, from small to large scale, founded by Xu Tiantian, winner of the WA China Architecture Award (2006) and the Young Architects Award of the Architectural League of New York (2008).

### Gage / Clemenceau Architects
Mark Foster Gage and Marc Clemenceau Bailly are the founders of Gage / Clemenceau Architects in New York City. The practice's work has been exhibited internationally at venues including the Museum of Modern Art in New York City, the Museum of the Art Institute of Chicago, and the Deutsches Architektur Zentrum in Berlin. The firm's design work was included in Icons of Graphic Design (2009) which lists the 'most influential designs and designers from 1900 to the present'.

### Ana Maria Reis de Goes Monteiro
Born in Brazil, graduated in architecture and city planning, and obtained a Masters in city planning from the Catholic Pontifical University of Campinas and a doctorate from the State University of Campinas. Professor of Architecture and City Planning at the State University of Campinas (UNICAMP), teaching and researching influences and perspectives in the formation and work of Brazilian architects and city planners.

### Kawamura-Ganjavian
Studio K+G is a young architecture studio established by Key Portilla-Kawamura and Ali Ganjavian in Madrid (2000). After meeting in London, where both were studying, they have undertaken professional and academic work in India, the USA, Japan, the UK, and Switzerland in the fields of urbanism, architecture, stage design, and product design.

**Kevin Le**

Born in Vietnam, graduated from Kansas State University and from Washington University. Employment: Canon Design (4 years), the Lawrence Group (9 years and counting). Married 11 years and blessed with 2 wonderful girls.

**Jan Leenknegt**

BS: KU Leuven, Architectural Engineering (1997). Masters: KU Leuven, Architectural Engineering (2000) and Columbia University, Architecture and Urban Design (2003). SOM Foundation Travel Fellowship for Urban Design (2003). Employment includes Studio Secchi-Vigano, KMDW, field Operations, SOM. Currently employed at SHoP Architects, New York.

**Filippo Lodi**

Born in Bologna, Italy. MSc Civil Engineering and Architecture at Alma Mater Studiorum, University of Bologna and University of Southampton. MA Advanced Architectural Design at Städelschule Hochschulde für Bildende Kunst, Frankfurt am Main. Currently residing in the Netherlands.

**Rebecca Luther**

Architect, urban designer, and educator. She received her Bachelor of Science in Architecture from the University of Virginia and her Master of Architecture from the Massachusetts Institute of Technology. For the past three years she was a lecturer in the Department of Architecture at MIT, teaching the Portfolio Seminar component of the recently expanded undergraduate architecture curriculum.

**Cathlyn Newell**

BS: Georgia Tech, Architecture (2003). Masters: Rice University, Architecture (2006). SOM Foundation Prize and Travel Fellowship for Architecture, Design and Urban Design (2006). Oberdick Fellow at University of Michigan (2009–10). Employment includes Office dA, Boston (2006–present).

**Openshop**

Founded in New York City by partners Adam Hayes and Mark Kroeckel (2000). The studio operates a process of research and design which is based on a fluid system of experimentation to address design problems of all sizes, shapes, and types.

**PellOverton**

An award-winning practice based in New York since 2003. The office has completed projects ranging in scale from exhibition design and gallery installations to small-scale building projects. Augmented by teaching and writing, the office examines contemporary questions of surface, materiality, and fabrication through various forms of practical research.

**Hilary Sample**

A principal of MOS, a collaborative design studio, and is an assistant professor at Yale University.

**Jennifer Silbert**

JSS8 is an interdisciplinary design firm focused on architecture, graphics, and film. Projects range in scale and scope, from complex architectural installations to logos and brand identity.

**Che-Wei Wang**

Born in Tokyo, to a Taiwanese mother and a Japanese/Taiwanese father, he has taught at the Pratt Institute School of Architecture at the University at Buffalo, Columbia University, University of Pennsylvania, and City College of New York. Che-Wei is the winner of the SOM Foundation fellowship (2003) and the Young Alumni Achievement Award at the Pratt Institute. He holds a B.Arch from the Pratt Institute and an MPS from ITP (TISCH NYU).

**Ceri Williams**
Born and brought up in Wales, studied
art before training at the Welsh School of
Architecture in Cardiff followed by the Royal
College of Art in London. He worked for two
years at Toh Shimazaki Architecture and
taught at their annual summer school, the t-sa
Forum. In 2009 he was included in Wallpaper
magazine's 'Graduate Directory'.

**Daniel J. Wolfe**
Born in Toledo, Ohio, gaines a BSc from
Bowling Green State University and Master
of Architecture from Southern California
Institute of Architecture. In 2007, worked as
an architectural designer at Patterns, a firm
located in West Hollywood California, on a
project known as 8746 Sunset Boutique:
the project is currently in the final phases of
construction. In the summer of 2008, served
as a guest instructor at Cal Poly of San Louis
Obispo. The seminar was titled 'Generative
Formations'.

**Richard M. Wright**
Senior Lecturer within the School of
Architecture at the University of Lincoln,
having previously taught at the Bartlett
School of Architecture and the University
of East London School of Architecture.
In tandem with his academic career has
constantly maintained a presence in
architectural practice, remaining a partner in
an architectural practice, with a modest but
relatively constant output of built works.

## Acknowledgements

This book would not have been possible without the shared experiences and candor of the contributors. I am inspired by their work and honoured by their participation. Many architecture and design professionals around the globe including students who inspired me have helped in different ways during the gestation of this book. Thank you to my wife, Frances Drew Elgood, for love, support, and editorial suggestions; my daughter Annabelle Drew Luescher, for her ideas of a portfolio as self-portrait; Francesca Ford, commissioning editor – architecture, for her interest in my work, keen wisdom, and steady advice; Faith McDonald, production editor, for keeping an eye on the manuscript and its swift realization; Penny Rogers, copy-editor, for her meticulous attention to detail; Georgina Johnson-Cook, assistant editor, for her guidance in the world of publishing; Jeffrey Hall, photographer, for creating the atmosphere on the cover of the book; Gavin Ambrose, book designer, for the lively format and spirited design; Theodore Cunningham, translator, for making the Portuguese contribution fluent in English; and Timothy A. Motz, at the Toledo Museum of Art, for invaluable information about Jean Tinguley.

# Index